T0146735

My True Love's Gifts

Rediscovering God in
"The Twelve Days of Christmas"

DAVID SAMFORD

WESTBOW
P R E S S®
A DIVISION OF THOMAS NELSON
& ZONDERVAN

Unless otherwise noted, Scripture quotations are taken from THE
HOLY BIBLE, NEW INTERNATIONAL VERSION®. NIV®,
Copyright © 1973, 1978, 1984, by International Bible Society. Used by
permission of Zondervan Publishing House. All rights reserved.

WestBow Press books may be ordered through booksellers or by contacting:

WestBow Press
A Division of Thomas Nelson & Zondervan
1663 Liberty Drive
Bloomington, IN 47403
www.westbowpress.com
1 (866) 928-1240

ISBN: 978-1-5127-9355-0 (sc)
ISBN: 978-1-5127-9356-7 (hc)
ISBN: 978-1-5127-9354-3 (e)

Library of Congress Control Number: 2017910929

Print information available on the last page.

WestBow Press rev. date: 7/31/2017

[A]nd it was always said of him, that he knew how to keep Christmas well, if any man alive possessed the knowledge. May that be truly said of us, and all of us!

—Charles Dickens, *A Christmas Carol*

But Mary treasured up all these things and pondered them in her heart.

—Luke 2:19

Contents

Acknowledgments

As with any project I undertake, the first acknowledgement is to my wife, Cheri. Her patience enabled me to write this book, and for that, I am profoundly grateful. Her thoughtful criticism really inspired me to write two books, the one in your hand and a companion volume that you will never read that is aptly entitled, *Twenty-Four Thousand Words at the Bottom of the Sea.* My children, Lillian and Harrison, are a constant source of encouragement and inspiration. They help me reconnect with the true spirit of Christmas every year.

Wayne opened his home and his heart to me at a couple of key points in the writing process. His insights on how to present the gospel of our Lord and Savior Jesus Christ are pearls of wisdom. I am also very appreciative of the comments and insights of everyone else who looked at the early and late drafts of the manuscript—Jeri, Jennifer, Sharon, Ben, Leanne, Stephanie, Michael, Morgan, Jon, Audra, Lisa, Allison, Tammy, David, and Gary. Stephanie and Mitch are the creative forces behind the cover. The entire team at WestBow Press has been a great blessing throughout the final stages of the project and a pleasure to work with. To all who were involved, I offer a sincere thank you. Your criticism was diplomatic. Your encouragement was sincere. Your friendship was genuine. An aspiring author can ask for nothing more.

Introduction

Rediscovering God in "The Twelve Days of Christmas"

Missing God at Christmas is like picking up your phone and seeing you just missed a call from your best friend.

Unfortunately, when most of us think of Christmas, we picture crowded stores, rude shoppers, traffic nightmares, and crazy schedules. We overeat, overspend and over decorate. It is all too easy to miss the point of the season entirely.

Christmastime has become a fifty-five day sprint from Halloween to Christmas Day. During that time, we are constantly urged and pushed to do things we normally would not do in a timeframe that is difficult to accomplish. We are so busy preparing for Christmas that finding time to read the Bible, pray, and enjoy our relationship with God is nearly impossible. How ironic that at one of the times of the year when we most want to feel God's presence, we are too preoccupied and distracted to do so.

Yet we enter into every new Christmas season hoping this will be the year we finally find time to focus on the true meaning of Christmas. When Christmas Day finally rolls around, however, these naive hopes often give way to the desperate, secret desire that it all might be over for one more year. "Next Christmas will be less stressful and more meaningful," we whisper to ourselves.

In the midst of a recent, hectic Christmas season, I rediscovered

God's presence in the most unexpected of places: a carol written about four hundred years ago. From as early as I can remember, "The Twelve Days of Christmas" was nothing more than an odd little song whose verses were easy to confuse and difficult to remember. Of course there are five golden rings, but are there seven drummers and eleven ladies dancing or, let me think, was it eleven pipers piping? I never really understood what the song had to do with Christmas. No one who worships Jesus Christ as their Lord and Savior would ever put this tune in the same category of meaningful Christmas carols such as "Joy to the World" and "Silent Night," right? "The Twelve Days of Christmas" falls somewhere on the spiritual significance meter between "Rudolph the Red-Nosed Reindeer" and "Grandma Got Run Over by a Reindeer."

Until one day the proverbial light bulb went off. There is a meaning to this song that is far greater than the superficial giving of unusual gifts. It reintroduced me to our Savior in a way that was profound and personal.

It seems we have been missing something. While scholars have written about the song, the true depth and meaning of "The Twelve Days of Christmas" has eluded most of us. The mystery begins with the fact that the "true love" is never identified. His name, nature, and intentions are never revealed and may only be discovered by considering the significance of the gifts he gives. Thus, in order to identify the true love, we must first understand the symbolic meaning of his gifts.

While this concept may at first seem mysterious, it is something we are already quite familiar with in our own experience. For instance, when we receive a gift card, we do not just receive a piece of plastic with a magnetic strip. We also have the ability to convert that card into a product or service that is tangible and valuable. If we fail to understand the symbolism of the gift card (represented by the merchant's logo and a dollar amount), then the gift is practically worthless. To get the most out of a gift card, we must understand that it points us to something that is greater and more valuable than just plastic. The same is true for "The Twelve Days of Christmas." When our true love gives a partridge in a pear tree, the gift points us toward something our true love also gives us that is far greater and more valuable than just a bird and a fruit tree.

The beauty of the carol is also found in the repetition of its verses. "The Twelve Days of Christmas" is a cumulative song, meaning that once a gift is given, the same gift is given on each of the following days of Christmas as well. The sum of the gifts given over the full twelve days includes twelve partridges and twelve pear trees, eleven pairs of calling birds, ten trios of French hens, and so forth. When Christmas is finally over, our true love's generosity amounts to a total of 364 gifts over the course of just twelve days! That is a lavish display of giving by any standard. In light of this generosity, "The Twelve Days of Christmas" provides the most comprehensive expression of what true love really means. It turns out that what I most desire at Christmas has been right here in front of me all this time.

If you have ever found the Christmas season to be an emotional and spiritual letdown, this book is for you. We are about to discover the real message in "The Twelve Days of Christmas" and experience Christmas from a perspective that is broader and deeper than the traditional nativity scene. We will discover something entirely new, inspiring, and encouraging in the words of a centuries-old lyric.

Joining in this journey requires accepting just one new gift from our true love per day, beginning on Christmas Day. As the amazing scope and extent of our true love's generosity is discovered, there will be no post-Christmas blues this year. I hope and pray that you will experience a lasting and genuine joy this Christmas season and, most importantly, that our true love's goodness and love will be clearly revealed. Once this occurs, you will be blessed and our true love will be most pleased.

December 25

A Partridge and a Pear Tree
Christmas – Christ with Us

On the first day of Christmas, my true love gave to me ...
A partridge in a pear tree.

Merry Christmas! Although Christmas sales started in July, today is the traditional first day of Christmas. The irony is quickly apparent. Just when we thought Christmas was over, it is really just beginning. That thought alone might be exhausting, because simply "making it through Christmas" sometimes becomes our primary objective for the holiday season. For many of us, the additional demands and expectations for decorating, cooking, performing, shopping, wrapping, and traveling are difficult to satisfy.

For others, those obligations are much preferable to the reality that Christmas can be a season of loneliness. For any number of reasons—sickness, divorce, death, or distance being just some of them—the last few weeks have been a constant reminder that this is the time of the year when we are expected to be joyful just because the calendar says so.

No matter our circumstances, we frequently miss the miracle of Christmas. We get so caught up in the cultural expectations of Christmas that we are simply too tired to actually experience and enjoy this time of year. We feel like little Cindy Lou Who in the movie *How the Grinch Stole Christmas* as she sings, "Where are you, Christmas?"

But not this year. Today marks the beginning of the most wonderful time of the year precisely because we are now free of the distractions and demands that very recently competed for our attention. Christmas starts today!

Yet it seems quite unusual that our true love gives us a partridge in a pear tree on the first day of Christmas. The gift reminds us of something we might get from someone who means well but who is pitifully out of touch with our needs and desires. Who has not opened an unexpected gift on Christmas Day and immediately said, "Oh, you *shouldn't* have ..."?

What are we to learn about our true love through the strange gift of a partridge and a pear tree? Once we understand the symbolic meaning of the gift, we discover that this is truly a remarkable present. In fact, this is the most precious blessing we could ever receive for Christmas. As my young son would say, "This is the best gift ever!"

You Can't Celebrate "Christmas" without a "Christ"

Before considering the symbolism of the partridge and the pear tree, we should first consider the importance of Christ to Christmas. The word Christ comes from a word that means anointed one. In ancient times, the words *Christ* (in Greek) and *messiah* (in Hebrew) were both used to describe someone who was anointed and set apart for a particular purpose or task. The word later began to have a special meaning. It became the title for the one person who would be set apart by God to redeem all humanity from the curses of sin. The Christ would be the Savior of the world.

God alone was recognized as the Savior throughout the Old Testament era. For instance, King David, a person who is said to have been very close to understanding God's heart, described God as the Savior on many occasions in Psalms. The prophet Isaiah was inspired to write, "Apart from [the LORD] there is no Savior" (Isa. 43:11). Elsewhere, God said, "There is no God apart from me, a righteous God and a Savior, there is none but me. Turn to me and be saved, all you ends of the earth; for I am God, and there is no other" (Isa. 45:21–22).

The Old Testament affirms the fundamental truth that people are incapable of saving themselves. A savior is necessary to rescue us from the consequences of our sins, and only God could be that savior. This notion is beautifully expressed in perhaps the most famous passage in the entire Bible, John 3:16, which says, "For God so loved the world that he gave his one and only Son, that whoever believes in him shall not perish but have eternal life."

God conceived his amazing plan to rescue us from the consequences of our sins even before he created the world. Paul writes, "This grace was given us in Christ Jesus *before the beginning of time*" (2 Tim. 1:9; emphasis added). In other words, even before God started making things, he understood that we would reject him and that the painful consequences of sin and death would follow. Nevertheless, God went ahead with his creation work, already having in mind an even greater plan to restore the broken relationship with each of us. That plan would begin in earnest on the very first Christmas Day.

But as all good holiday planners know, an awesome Christmas requires careful preparation. So God immediately started dropping hints and clues about how and when that first Christmas would come about. He first warned the serpent in the Garden of Eden that sin's curses would be undone by an offspring of woman—a human (Gen. 3:15). God later told Abraham that a blessing for all nations would come from his descendants (Gen. 12:3). God then inspired Jacob to proclaim that the role of leadership would be reserved for the tribe of Judah (Gen. 49:10). God told King David hundreds of years later, "Your house and your kingdom will endure forever before me; your throne will be established forever" (2 Sam.

7:16). The prophet Micah foretold, "But you, Bethlehem Ephrathah, though you are small among the clans of Judah, out of you will come for me one who will be ruler over Israel, whose origins are from of old, from ancient times" (Mic. 5:2). Isaiah prophesied that the Christ would be born of a virgin (Isa. 7:14). The Old Testament ends with us eagerly anticipating the Christ's arrival.

Fast-forward another four hundred years to a ho-hum night in a sleepy little village in Israel. This is the familiar context for our thoughts about Christmas, with Mary and Joseph as the weary travelers seeking refuge during the final days of a scandalous pregnancy. Then, with all the pomp and circumstance of a county fair, cattle and donkeys find themselves standing as boisterous witnesses to the birth of the baby.

Shepherds soon arrive, speaking excitedly about a choir of angels that appeared in the sky and sang of the fulfillment of ancient prophecies. And later, just when things could not possibly get more bizarre, officials from a distant land arrive and worship the young child, present him with expensive gifts, and call him a king.

This seems like such an impossible backdrop for setting God's plan of salvation into its most critical phase, but we must remember another of God's statements: "For my thoughts are not your thoughts, neither are your ways my ways" (Isa. 55:8).

With the benefit of hindsight, we are not nearly as surprised as the shepherds were when angels appeared in the sky and proclaimed, "Today in the town of David a Savior has been born to you; he is Christ the Lord" (Luke 2:11). We know that Jesus's birth fit the prophecies perfectly. He was a human, and he was also a descendant of Abraham, Judah, and David. He was born to a virgin in the little town of Bethlehem. Even the visit of the wise men was foretold in Psalm 95:6–7, which says, "Come, let us bow down in worship, let us kneel before the LORD our Maker, for he is our God and we are the people of his pasture, the flock under his care."

To be the true Christ, Jesus had to be God; this was a fact affirmed by Peter, who passionately proclaimed that Jesus "is the Christ, the son of the living God" (Matt. 16:36). When the Samaritans heard Jesus speak, they agreed that "this man really is the Savior of the world" (John 4:42). Jesus claimed to be the Christ many times, and Peter, Paul, and John referred to him as the Christ over four hundred times in their letters. Jesus is our Savior. He is the Christ in Christmas.

The Partridge

Now, about that partridge. There are three characteristics that make partridges different from most other bird species. First, partridges prefer to make their nests on the ground, not in trees. Second, partridges are fiercely territorial. When they make a nest, they protect it aggressively. Third, partridges make a commitment to their mates that is unusual among animals. Male and female partridges both take part in protecting their eggs and nurturing their young, not just for one season but over multiple seasons. These same three qualities are all characteristics represented in our true love's first gift. The partridge is symbolic of Jesus.

Jesus Gave Up the Sanctuary of the Heavens

As a partridge chooses to give up the sanctuary of the trees and the skies, Jesus chose to come down from heaven and make his nest in the hills of Palestine.

The idea of God going from heaven to earth is present in both the Old Testament and the New Testament, but the context between these two eras is quite different. In the Old Testament, God says he will "go down" to confuse the language of those who disobey his commands (Gen. 11:5). A similar scene occurs in Exodus when God comes down from heaven to give the law to Moses atop Mount Sinai (Ex. 32:15). God's trips from heaven to earth in the Old Testament mostly have to do with punishing disobedience or giving instructions.

In the New Testament, God comes to earth for a very different purpose. In John 6:33, Jesus describes himself as "the bread of God ... who comes down from heaven and gives life to the world." Looking forward to Jesus's return, Paul wrote, "For the Lord himself will come down from heaven" (1 Thess. 4:16). The fact that Jesus would leave heaven to live among us makes Christmas an annual reminder of just how precious we are to God.

Jesus Protects What Is His

Jesus also confused his critics by being so protective of those who trusted him. When opponents accused him of breaking the law, Jesus said he came to fulfill the law (Matt. 5:17), a task no ordinary person could ever hope to accomplish. When he was accused of spending time with cheaters, prostitutes, and drunks, Jesus said that was exactly what he planned to do because they were the people most willing to accept his friendship (Mark 2:15–17). When he visited the temple, Jesus eagerly overturned the tables of those who profited from the rituals of worship by exploiting the faithful (John 2:13–17). Paul explains Jesus's purpose when he writes, "Here is a trustworthy saying that deserves full acceptance: Christ Jesus came into the world to save sinners—of whom I am the worst" (1 Tim. 1:14).

Jesus's commitment to protect and restore the glory of creation is the defining characteristic of his earthly life. In John 10:11, he says, "I am the good shepherd. The good shepherd lays down his life for the sheep." In Luke 19:10, Jesus says he "came to seek and save what was lost," and in John 3:17, he says, "God did not send his Son into the world to condemn the world, but to save the world through him." Jesus constantly explained that he was reversing the consequences of sin and saving what Satan sought to destroy (Matt. 12:25–28).

Jesus's life is proof that God never abandoned humanity to

Satan's snares. God sent his Son to protect us and restore our broken relationships.

Jesus Commits to Relationships that Last

The relationship Jesus desires to have with each of us is so personal and long-lasting that even the apostle Paul had trouble fully explaining it. Sometimes he described our relationship to Jesus as one of kinship, as we become sons and daughters of God and heirs to his kingdom (Rom. 8:17). Other times it is described as the ideal marriage, where the husband and wife routinely put the interests of the other ahead of their own (Eph. 5:23).

The fact that there is no perfect illustration to demonstrate the depth of Jesus's love for us is an incredible thought all by itself. Paul embraced the reality that God's love was greater than we could possibly imagine by writing, "And I pray that you, being rooted and established in love, may have power ... to grasp how wide and long and high and deep is the love of Christ, and to know this love that surpasses knowledge, that you may be filled to the measure of all of the fullness of God" (Eph. 3:17–19).

The most exciting thing is that we share our personal relationship with Jesus with fellow believers. Jesus established the church to be the community of his followers, united upon the truth that he is the Christ, the Son of God. Our relationship to Jesus and fellow believers lasts forever.

The Pear Tree

The pear tree adds another beautiful layer of symbolism to our true love's first gift. You can think of the pear tree as being just like the double-wrapped package that, as you open it, you see holds another box containing the real gift.

As much as we want to focus on Christ's birth on Christmas Day, the real gift is where Christ is found in our carol. Our true love doesn't give us Christ in a manger. Instead, he gives us Jesus on a tree.

Our true love is thinking about what Paul preached to his countrymen: "When they had carried out all that was written about [Jesus], *they took him down from the tree* and laid him in a tomb" (Acts 13:29; emphasis added). Jesus allowed himself to be nailed to a wooden cross as the punishment for all of humanity's sins. There can be no greater gift than this.

Our true love's first gift unmistakably associates Jesus Christ with the cross. We celebrate the first day of Christmas by marking Jesus's birth while also anticipating the purpose of that birth. The supreme importance of this gift is emphasized by the fact that it is the only gift our true love gives on every day of the Christmas season.

We miss the most sacred aspect of Christmas Day if all we see is a manger scene. Our true love's first gift reminds us that Jesus came to earth knowing he would one day be nailed to a cross. Yet, through this crucifixion, the restoration of all things would again be possible and the process of reversing sin's curses could finally begin. Without the tree that was roughly fashioned into a cross, the value and significance of Christmas would be diminished. Easter celebrates the day that Jesus walked out of the tomb and conquered death, but it is today, Christmas Day, that makes Easter possible.

Reflection

The first day of Christmas is about the Christ. It reminds us that our Christmas activities are insignificant and meaningless if they are based only upon artificial traditions. To experience a real Christmas, we must have a real Christ, a Savior who is personal, trustworthy, and powerful. This Savior must love us so greatly that he would allow himself to become vulnerable, first as a baby and then as the perfect sacrifice for every ugly sin that haunts us. All of this is necessary in order to save us from ourselves and restore the relationship God desires with each of us.

This is the first day of Christmas, the day when we acknowledge and celebrate the giving of our true love's greatest gift, the Christ and the cross. It is an invitation to have a personal relationship with Jesus, the Savior of the world.

And we still have eleven more blessings to unwrap! Our true love's next gift gives further meaning and depth to the gift we received today. It places the miracle of Christmas Day within the context of a much bigger and more exciting journey.

As children went to bed last evening with happy expectations of what today would bring, it is my hope that you have that same sense of eagerness right now. Our true love's next gift is waiting.

December 26

Two Turtledoves
The Bible – Two Testaments of God's Love

On the second day of Christmas, my true love gave to me ...
Two turtledoves and a partridge in a pear tree.

Our true love's gift for Christmas Day was perfect, the promised Christ and the rugged cross. But not all gifts are accepted. Today is the day when millions of Christmas gifts are rejected, returned, and forgotten.

Retailers know this and open their stores early to accept the flood of gifts that were impractical, ill-fitting, or just not to our liking. They also just happen to have plenty of other items available for sale as Christmas markdowns. You might even find an early sale on Valentine's Day merchandise.

Rejection is a big part of the Christmas season. Although we say "it is the thought that counts," the era of no-hassle returns tempts us to measure the value of each gift by the standards of our own desires more than the intentions of the giver. It is very easy to exchange someone's thoughtful gift of a sweater for something we "really want."

Amidst the race to the customer service desk, we should recall that our true love gives gifts over twelve days instead of lavishing all of them in just one day. The clear implication is that we should accept all our true love's gifts before we decide to reject any single one of them. Our true love's generosity is also measured by its duration, not just by its magnitude.

So what do the two turtledoves we receive today tell us about our true love? Throughout the Bible, doves are associated with God's work. From the sacrifice of doves as a sin offering to the Holy Spirit's manifestation as a dove at Jesus's baptism, these birds are a sign that God is active. The best record of God's activities throughout history is the Bible, which is itself divided into two parts—the Old Testament and the New Testament. Our true love's turtledoves are a symbolic expression of these two testaments.

The Old Testament and New Testament help us better understand yesterday's gift, Jesus Christ and the cross, because they are the "before" and the "after" of Jesus's ministry. They describe why Jesus was born and what his life means for each of us. Working together, the Old Testament and the New Testament explain the who, the what, the when, the where, and the why of God's love for each of us.

The Old Testament

The Old Testament records the period of history that begins with creation and ends about four centuries before Jesus's birth. The Old Testament's thirty-nine books are an impressive collection of ancient writings that may be divided into two broad categories— the Law and the Prophets. Jesus himself referred to this distinction (Matt. 7:12). However, the Old Testament may also be divided into another division that includes five books of law, twelve books of history, five books of wisdom, five Major Prophets, and twelve Minor Prophets.

The Books of Law

Genesis, Exodus, Leviticus, Numbers, and Deuteronomy are sometimes referred to as the Pentateuch, a Greek word meaning "five books." These books introduce us to God and explain why it was necessary for Jesus to come to earth and die as a sacrifice for our sins.

In the first part of Genesis, we see that God intended to live in the presence of humanity, surrounded by a perfect creation. The sin of Adam and Eve in the Garden of Eden spoiled the plan, however, and the consequences of their sin negatively changed the course of history for both humanity and creation. But as we saw yesterday, God was already implementing his plan to save us and restore creation.

God's plan to rescue us from our sins took a giant step forward when Abraham obeyed God's command to travel to a distant, unknown land. Abraham's obedience set in motion a series of events through which some of his descendants became the nation of Israel. The troubles Israel faced as a nation demonstrated that no one can save themselves from the consequences of sin. Israel was incapable of following just a few rules given by God. The Christ was needed to save Israel, and all of us.

The Books of History

The next twelve books recount the history of the Israelites from the time they first entered the Promised Land through the time they are restored to the Promised Land after a seventy-year exile. Israel is first blessed by God for obedience to his commands, but these blessings cause Israel to become arrogant. That arrogance leads the people to ignore God and then actively disobey him. Israel's rebellion results in punishment from God, which reminds the people of their sins. When the Israelites apologize for their wickedness and change their behavior, God forgives them and blesses his people once again. And then Israel becomes arrogant once more and the cycle tragically repeats.

Some of the most fascinating characters of the Bible are included in these books. Joshua, Gideon, David, Solomon, Esther, and Nehemiah are all good leaders, but none of them is perfect and each must confront personal doubts and deal with mistakes. Samuel, Elijah, and Elisha serve as mighty prophets, but much of their wisdom is ignored.

These stories offer revealing insights into human nature. Jezebel is a model of wickedness. Deborah is a wonderful example of courage. Some of the best examples of faithfulness unexpectedly come from non-Israelites such as Ruth and Naaman. It seems that human nature has not changed over the course of the last four thousand years. These ancient heroes and villains have the exact same thoughts and attitudes we have today.

God is faithful through it all. He welcomes his people whenever they turn away from sin. Most importantly, God is actively working to accomplish his plan to save us.

The Books of Wisdom

Job, Psalms, Proverbs, Ecclesiastes, and the Song of Solomon are the Old Testament's wisdom literature. These books showcase human emotions and attitudes in a variety of circumstances. Job tells the story of a man who suffered in every way possible. He struggled with illness, the death of loved ones, financial ruin, doubts, fears, and anxieties. His questions about God's nature were legitimate, but God answered them by posing his own questions to Job. While this might seem evasive, Job's conversation with God fortified his faith and reduced his suffering. Job's patience was rewarded and God's awesome nature was revealed through later events.

Psalms is a collection of poems and hymns covering the full spectrum of human experiences and emotions. We read of the joy of basking in the Lord's delight as well as the crushing weight of being relentlessly pursued by enemies intent on destruction and mayhem. The Psalms are a window into the emotions of our own hearts, making them some of the most frequently recited passages of the Old Testament.

Proverbs, Ecclesiastes, and the Song of Solomon were mostly prepared by Solomon. Proverbs explains why wisdom is valuable and contains a lengthy collection of sayings on topics such as money, relationships, and priorities. Ecclesiastes follows as an extended meditation on the meaning of life. It concludes that the only true fulfillment in life comes from accurately understanding our relationship to God and acting accordingly. This reflective book is followed by the Song of Solomon, which describes the lives of two passionate lovers in a level of detail that would make Hollywood's film rating experts blush. The Song of Solomon is an allegorical description of God's intense desire to have a relationship with each of us. Solomon's writings probe the deepest questions surrounding God's nature and the meaning of life.

The Major Prophets

Isaiah, Jeremiah, Lamentations, Ezekiel, and Daniel are the Major Prophets. Their "major" status is derived simply from the fact that they are generally lengthier than the Minor Prophets.

The defining event in these books is the destruction of Israel and its exile, which is the result of centuries of disobedience to God. Isaiah repeatedly warns the people living in Jerusalem that they will follow their brothers into exile if their relationship to God does not improve. The destruction of Jerusalem comes to pass during the time of Jeremiah, who both warns the people to repent on the eve of an invasion by the Babylonians and then weeps over the destruction of Jerusalem a short time later in Lamentations.

Ezekiel and Daniel are written during the period of the exile and in anticipation of better days to come. Ezekiel foresees that God will resurrect the nation of Israel and restore it to the Promised

Land. Daniel looks further into the future and foretells the rise of three future empires—the Persians, the Greeks, and the Romans—who will come to dominate the course of world history over the next thousand years. His prophecies in Daniel 11 are so accurate that he precisely describes the intense civil war that will break out following the death of Alexander the Great, who had not yet even been born.

Despite a persistent sense of regret and sorrow, the Major Prophets also contain a constant message of hope and optimism. Even in the darkest moments, God still speaks words of encouragement to his people. Nothing can derail God's plan to save us. It is coming closer and closer to fruition.

The Minor Prophets

The twelve Minor Prophets round out the Old Testament and, in terms of chronology, overlap with the books of history and the Major Prophets. These prophets also gave several warnings to Israel that God's judgment would not be delayed forever and that disobedience would result in judgment.

The books uniquely include warnings to other nations as well. Obadiah warns the Edomites that they will be punished for aiding Israel's enemies. Jonah warns the Ninevites that they are about to be destroyed for their wickedness. When they seek forgiveness, God withholds punishment. Jonah is sorely disappointed that Nineveh is not destroyed, leading God to point out Jonah's poor attitude. Later, however, the Ninevites refuse to listen to Nahum's new warnings and judgment follows.

The Minor Prophets continue to bring the need for a Christ into sharper focus. Obadiah, Jonah, and Nahum demonstrate that this need is not isolated to Israel alone. It is a universal need shared by all nations and all generations.

The Old Testament ends with a cliff-hanger. The Christ is coming, but we don't know when. Four hundred years of silence separate the end of the Old Testament from the final preparations for the birth of Jesus Christ in Bethlehem in the New Testament.

The New Testament

The New Testament begins with an angel foretelling of the births of John the Baptist and Jesus. It then describes the life of Jesus as recorded in the four Gospels, one book of history, twenty-one letters written by some of Jesus's closest followers, and one final book of prophecy. The New Testament explains the life and ministry of Jesus, gives us practical guidance for living our lives, and assures us that the curses of sin will ultimately be undone when the world is restored to its original design.

The Four Gospels of Jesus Christ

Matthew, Mark, Luke, and John provide eyewitness accounts of the life of Jesus Christ. Each of these books is written from the unique perspective of its author, adding richness to the text and flavor to the details of every event that is recorded.

The Gospels reveal God's nature. They tell how Jesus fulfilled the Old Testament prophecies concerning the Christ. They describe how he lived a simple life characterized by humility, service, and sacrifice. These books record his wisdom and teachings. The Gospels also tell us about the countless miracles Jesus performed in wedding halls, along city streets, atop crowded mountains, and in the midst of raging storms.

They are the foundation of our faith as Christians because they describe the kingdom of God and tell us how to imitate Jesus's lifestyle. For this reason, our true love will re-emphasize the importance of the Gospels with another gift in just a couple of days.

The History of the Holy Spirit

Acts is the New Testament's only history book. It describes the Holy Spirit's work in the early days of the church. The Holy Spirit's power helps the community of Jesus's followers to grow rapidly in Jerusalem. When this causes opponents to persecute the growing church, the Christians flee and take the gospel message with them. They travel throughout nearby lands and neighboring regions.

Later, Jesus appears to a man named Saul, who discovers that his efforts to kill Christians are misguided and wrong. Saul's name is changed to Paul and he becomes one of the greatest missionaries of the first century. In addition to the thousands of miles he walks and sails, Paul writes over a dozen letters to Christians scattered throughout the Roman Empire.

The Twenty-One Letters of Paul, Peter, James, John, and Jude

The dominant style of writing in the New Testament takes the form of letters written by the early apostles to the churches they helped establish and the leaders they helped grow in the faith. These twenty-one letters are encouraging and instructive. They also give warnings to those who would corrupt the gospel message. The letters reflect the wildly different personalities of their authors and the cultural diversity of the churches themselves, but they uniformly help us know Jesus more personally. We see that the earliest believers' spiritual struggles are no different than the challenges and temptations we face today. The instructions and encouragement these early Christians received are still quite relevant. The faithfulness of the first generation of Jesus's followers gives us an example to follow and offers hope that we too may remain faithful.

One Book of Prophecy

The New Testament concludes with Revelation, a book of prophecy. The only prophecy about Jesus that remains unfilled is that he will return to earth to bring a final judgment upon the world. Those who love him will be resurrected to eternal life in heaven. Those who reject him will not be so blessed.

Revelation describes the future in a series of visions experienced by John, Jesus's closest friend during his brief ministry. The language of Revelation is confusing to modern readers, partly because we often try to interpret it based upon the history of the world that has occurred since John's exile. This is probably unnecessary. The meaning that the first readers of Revelation would have understood is likely still the best meaning we could discern today.

Revelation is not intended to be a calendar for predicting Jesus's return nearly so much as it is a source of encouragement and affirmation that his return will one day occur. Knowing that Jesus will return means we accept that God is in control of history. We may face the uncertainties of life without surrendering to fear and anxiety because we are convinced the future holds no real danger. The pain we must sometimes endure is exceedingly outweighed by the joy of knowing we will spend eternity in God's presence.

Reflection

Many Christmas gifts were rejected and forgotten today. Indeed, the nature of a gift is such that it must be accepted in order to truly be received. Our true love's first gift, the Christ and his cross, is given again today. But it also comes with two testaments to God's work. These testaments demonstrate how God has been active throughout history to save us from ourselves and, ultimately, how he will restore our perfect relationship with him. Yesterday's invitation to have a personal relationship with Jesus has become more specific. The invitation now has context that describes exactly what is at stake.

Will we accept our true love's first two gifts, or do we prefer to exchange them for something we think is more desirable?

Unsurprisingly, our true love anticipates this question and his next gift promises to show us there is nothing more desirable than having a personal, genuine relationship with Jesus. On the third day of Christmas, our true love promises to give us the three virtues necessary to live a meaningful, well-lived life. What can be more desirable than that?

Christmas has just begun.

December 27

Three French Hens
Faith, Hope, and Love – The Good Life

On the third day of Christmas, my true love gave to me ...
Three french hens,
Two turtledoves, and a partridge in a pear tree.

With Christmas Day now two days behind us, things are different. Christmas dinner has turned into leftovers. Pretty wrapping paper and bows are sitting on the curb in garbage bags. Extended families that united for Christmas are beginning to make their way back to distant homes. Some folks are already talking about undecorating. There are no more Christmas songs on the radio. How dreadful!

Christmas experiences are becoming Christmas memories. We all know what comes next. It is time for a case of the "post-Christmas blues."

After all the excitement leading up to Christmas, an emotional letdown inevitably follows. Did we make the most of this Christmas? Will we remember it a few years from now? How can Christmas continue in our hearts when every reminder of the season is out on the curb or going back into the closet?

Today, we are even more intrigued with the notion that Christmas is not over, because all of the evidence tells us otherwise.

Today's gift from our true love must therefore be more powerful than emotions and perceptions. It must be significant enough to conquer the doldrums.

At first blush, three French hens would appear to be just another odd gift. What can three little birds possibly tell us about our true love? Equally perplexing is this question: what do three French hens have to do with Jesus Christ or the Bible?

To understand the meaning and value of our latest gift, we should know that French hens were a delicacy only the wealthy and affluent could afford at the time "The Twelve Days of Christmas" was written. They were a source of food reserved for those who lived "the good life." It is the idea of living a good life that is symbolized in our true love's third gift. Specifically, a well-lived life is characterized by possessing three important virtues: faith, hope, and love (1 Cor. 13:13). Three French hens are the perfect symbolic expression of our true love's desire to help us live the best life possible.

Faith

We get on an airplane because we have faith in the pilots, air traffic controllers, and aerodynamic engineers. We do not personally know that a model airframe was tested in a wind tunnel, that the wing's rivets are secure, that the pilots are trained, or even that there are controllers in the tower, but we trust and believe these critical elements of flight are true. If we did not have such faith, we would likely never step onto the airplane.

Everyone has faith in something, but that is not what is important in life. To live the good life, our faith has to be properly placed. We must have faith in something that will not fail.

Hebrews 11:1 says "faith is being sure of what we hope for and certain of what we do not see." The passage goes on to list many examples of genuine faith on display in the Bible. These heroes began journeys to unknown destinations, stared down hungry lions, stood in a fiery furnace, and accepted hardships and persecutions. When we say we have faith, what we are really saying is that we accept something as true even when we cannot fully explain it or completely understand it.

And that is a good thing. I could never fully understand everything Jesus did or explain all of the chapters of the Bible, but I know that Jesus is my Savior and that the Bible is God's inspired message. The first part of today's gift reminds us that just having a little faith is enough to please God.

Hebrews 11:6 says, "And without faith it is impossible to please God, because anyone who comes to him must believe that he exists and that he rewards those who earnestly seek him." This brief verse offers a wonderful blessing. We are not required to put our faith in complex doctrines, church traditions, charismatic leaders, or repetitive religious rituals. Faith is rooted in nothing more than the belief that God exists and that he rewards those who seek him. In order to have genuine faith, we need only to understand that there is a God and we should look for him.

Believing God exists should not be particularly difficult. Paul writes, "For since the creation of the world God's invisible qualities—his eternal power and divine nature—have been clearly seen, being understood from what has been made, so that men are without excuse" (Rom. 1:20). God reveals the fact of his existence every day. He does it through such things as the vast structures of the universe, the physical processes of the earth, and the complexities of the human body.

Simple observation tells us these realities are not accidents of chance. The universe we live in gives us more than enough information to know there is a God. Yet knowing he exists is not the same as being certain as to what God is like. For example, I know that if I follow the sun in the evening, it will lead me toward the west, but the progression of the sun alone will not lead me to the exact address of my destination.

The good news is that God promises to reward those who look

for him. This was just as true in Jesus's time as it is in ours. As an example, Jesus singles out the faith of a Roman military officer who has enough faith to believe Jesus could restore health to his servant simply by commanding it. From the officer's perspective, there is no need for Jesus to even visit the sick servant. Jesus reacts to this dramatic profession of faith by saying, "I tell you the truth, I have not found anyone in Israel with such great faith" (Matt. 8:10).

The officer's request was based upon his faith that it is God's nature to have compassion upon the sick. The officer's faith was greatly rewarded, as his servant was immediately restored to health. A small amount of faith can lead to an amazing miracle that produces even greater faith. When others showed similar faith in him, Jesus healed a paralytic man, cured a woman of chronic bleeding, restored sight to blind men, healed a woman's daughter, cleansed a man of leprosy, and gave forgiveness for sins. These miracles are just a few of the highlights of Jesus's ministry.

God values our efforts to discover his character, because the journey reveals God's willingness to forgive our sins. Paul expands upon this idea when he writes, "we have peace with God through our Lord Jesus Christ, through whom we have gained access by faith into this grace in which we now stand" (Rom. 5:1–2). By reminding us of the virtue of faith, our true love is inviting us to seek God and to enjoy the reward of grace that follows.

Hope

Hope is another virtue essential to living a good life. Like faith, hope is also a universal quality because everyone has hope in something. Hope is one thing that can never be taken away by someone else. It is only lost when it is given up and surrendered.

Nowhere is this concept more vividly illustrated than in the story of Job. The word "hope" appears eighteen times in the book of Job alone. At the beginning of his story, Job is described as "the greatest man among all the peoples of the East." Job has great wealth, vast flocks and herds, and many fine children. Then all of it is lost in a swift series of catastrophes. Job's friends come to comfort him, but they rationalize his unexpected misery by blaming him for somehow bringing this disaster upon himself. Job's wife tells him to curse God and die so that his despair and suffering will come to an end.

Despite this "encouragement," Job accepts the events that have turned his world upside down as being part of God's plan. In fact, the reader of Job has the benefit of knowing that Job's misfortunes are indeed part of a larger, unseen drama. What is so remarkable about Job, however, is that his hope in God never fails, even in the midst of great loss and personal tragedy. In Job 13:15, we read, "Though he slay me, yet will I hope in him" Job would accept death as the price of maintaining his hope in God. Job's faith enabled him to have a genuine hope that was greater than his own understanding of the awful circumstances he faced.

The hope of Job is even more inspiring when we put this man's story within the larger context of the entire Bible. Job was not a descendant of Abraham, Isaac, and Jacob. As such, he was not a part of God's covenant with those patriarchs. He did not have the benefit of experiencing God's power in Egypt, at Sinai, or in the wilderness. Job did not rely upon passages from the Psalms because they had not yet been written. Job's hope in God was based purely upon his personal relationship with God.

Hope ripples across the Old Testament. In Psalm 33, David sings of how Israel placed its hope in God. Jeremiah goes so far as to use "Hope" as a name for God (Jer. 17:13). In Psalm 119, David personally puts his hope in the word of God. The value of well-placed hope is illustrated in Isaiah 40:31, a passage highlighted in the 1981 Academy Award-winning movie *Chariots of Fire*, which says, "Those who hope in the LORD will renew their strength. They will soar on wings like eagles; they will run and not grow weary, they will walk and not be faint."

Hope sets the stage for the New Testament as well. Paul

explains that one of the Old Testament's purposes was to give hope to future generations. "For everything that was written in the past was written to teach us, so that through endurance and the encouragement of the Scriptures we might have hope" (Rom. 15:4). The value of hope in our lives is magnified in the New Testament. We place our hope in God (1 Tim. 6:17), his glory (Rom. 5:2), the redemption of our bodies (Rom. 8:23), the return of Jesus Christ (Titus 2:13), the grace that will be shown to us on that day (1 Pet. 1:13), and eternal life (Titus 1:2, 3:7). When we do this, Paul tells us that our hope will produce joy (Rom. 12:12), boldness (2 Cor. 3:12), patience (Rom. 8:25), and endurance (1 Thess. 1:3). It is no wonder that Hebrews 6:19 describes hope as "an anchor for our soul, firm and secure."

Focusing our hopes upon the goodness of God's will puts us in the same company as Job, Ruth, David, Isaiah, Jeremiah, Daniel, Esther, Paul, and others who navigated through perils and challenges. That is the point of view expressed in Lamentations 3:21–24, which says, "Yet this I call to mind and therefore I have hope: Because of the LORD's great love we are not consumed, for his compassions never fail. They are new every morning; great is your faithfulness." The gift of hope is a wonderful gift on the third day of Christmas, a powerful reminder that God's love is renewed each time we take a breath.

Love

Love is the third virtue essential to living a good life. In fact, Paul calls love the greatest virtue of them all (1 Cor. 13:13). So is this where we cue Shaggy and the Big Yard Family to sing that reggae Christmas classic, "All We Need Is Love"? As much as I miss it on the radio already, not quite yet.

The love Paul is talking about is more than just our affection for a friend or our passion for a lover. To understand what Paul means, we must return to the era when people mostly spoke Greek, the language of Socrates, Plato, and Aristotle. Unlike English, where the meaning of a word must sometimes be determined based upon its context and usage, the ancient Greeks used different words to describe different types of love.

For example, *eros* is the Greek word most often used to describe intimate or romantic love. The English equivalent would be the word "erotic." Likewise, the Greeks used a different word, *phileo*, to describe love that is based upon a friendly relationship. Philadelphia is for this reason known as the "City of Brotherly Love." While *eros* and *phileo* are appropriate to describe many of the encounters we have with love in popular culture, neither of them is the word that is actually translated as "love" throughout most of the New Testament.

The New Testament conception of love is much, much deeper. The love that Jesus shows us, and that we are asked to show others, is *agape* in Greek. *Agape* is not an emotional form of love. This makes it a difficult idea to comprehend. *Agape* is a love based upon the conscious choice of the lover to express love and not upon the loveliness of the person being loved. *Agape* is an intentional form of love that arises solely within the will and intentions of the person expressing the love. It matters not whether the object of that expression of love is attractive or a family member.

When Paul sought to describe *agape* to the Corinthians (1 Cor. 13), he wrote that it is patient, kind, protective, trusting, truthful, hopeful, perseverant, and eternal. But he also defined this form of love by what it is not. *Agape* is not envious, boastful, proud, rude, selfish, quickly angered, begrudging, or delighting in evil. *Agape* cannot be corrupted or watered down, because it is the definition of true love.

For over fifteen years, our church has led a ministry to serve a hot meal to the homeless on Sunday afternoons. No one who is served pays for the meal. From start to finish, this simple ministry is an example of *agape* love.

Agape is modeled for us in the conscious choice of Jesus Christ to leave heaven and to walk among us—healing, teaching, and saving as he went—before ultimately allowing himself to be crucified as the perfect sacrifice for our sins. When we imitate Christ's love for us, we find ourselves meeting the needs of others simply because their needs exist. Such actions are the perfect expression of living the good life.

Reflection

We already have Jesus and the cross to save us from our sins and the Bible to guide our lives. As wonderful as those gifts may be, those gifts are only a prelude to our true love's newest gift. They give us the context we need to properly place our faith and hope in God alone and to imitate his *agape* style of love for us in our encounters with others. It is no mistake that faith, hope, and love come to us on the same day. They are the virtues through which we might live a good life, as God intended. They also provide the first tantalizing glimpse of the many blessings that our true love still has in store for those who accept the invitation to have a personal relationship with Jesus.

Each day we learn a little bit more about our true love's character and nature, but he has not yet revealed himself fully. In fact, our true love has nine more gifts to bestow. Beginning tomorrow, our true love's gifts will begin to draw us even closer to his heart by revealing his thoughts and attitudes in increasing degrees of detail. The great lengths he will go to in order to demonstrate his love for us have yet to be revealed, but they are ready to be unwrapped.

Our true love's desire to win our hearts is more and more apparent each day of this Christmas season. Another new gift is coming. This thought alone banishes the post-Christmas blues.

December 28

Four Calling Birds
The Gospels – Jesus Revealed

On the fourth day of Christmas, my true love gave to me ...
Four calling birds,
Three French hens, two turtledoves, and a partridge in a pear tree.

Today is the "hump day" of the holiday season. Christmas was three days ago and New Year's Eve is three days from now. The constant barrage of "look back" and "year in review" programs remind us we need a new calendar. Now is also the time to start thinking seriously about what we want to accomplish next year. Television, radio, and blogs are filled with folks making their predictions for what the coming year holds for politics, the economy, entertainment, fashion, pop culture, and technology. Apparently, the new smart phone I just bought in October will be obsolete and replaced by a newer model in March.

The task of reminiscing and predicting is not our true love's fourth gift. His attention is exclusively focused on nurturing what we have already been given, which is this: a growing, personal relationship with Jesus, our Lord and Savior. Our relationship with Jesus comes to the forefront on the fourth day of Christmas in the form of four calling birds.

If you have ever heard the tweet-tweets of a songbird in the morning, the prattling of a gobbling turkey, or the echoing cry of a raven in the forest, you know that a bird's voice is distinctive and attention-grabbing. A person with a trained ear can name the species of a bird simply by hearing its voice. Calling birds in particular make their presence known by projecting their voices over great distances.

Our true love's fourth gift is symbolic of four books that have similarly echoed a message of good news over the pages of history for two thousand years. Today's gift of four calling birds is symbolic of the four Gospels—Matthew, Mark, Luke, and John.

Though we first encountered the Gospels two days ago when our true love presented us with the New Testament, at that point they were only part of God's much larger message for humanity. By giving the Gospels all by themselves, our true love is emphasizing the importance of the man whose life dominates all four books. That man, of course, is Jesus Christ.

Yet each of the Gospels also describes the unique experiences and perspectives of the four authors who wrote the "good news" (the meaning of the word "gospel"). In comparing these accounts, we find some events in Jesus's life are only recorded in one of the Gospels, while other events are documented in all of them. Just like four different species of birds will announce the arrival of morning in their own distinctive voice, the four Gospels each announce a new relationship between God and humanity in their own distinctive way. We see a more comprehensive picture of the man who most greatly changed the course of history by reading these four books together. The Gospels provide a unified narrative of the time when God became a man so that we could know him and become part of his family.

Matthew

Matthew was a tax collector for Rome, the foreign power that occupied and ruled over Israel in the first century. His chosen career was well suited to acquiring material wealth. With the authority of the Roman Empire behind him, Matthew could collect whatever taxes he thought his countrymen should pay. Opportunities for corruption and mischief were always present. Tax collectors such as Matthew were despised by the Israelites, who regarded them as traitors.

Matthew would have been especially disliked because his Hebrew name was Levi. He was named after the leader of the tribe of Israel that was entrusted to serve as God's priests. In Genesis, the Levites distinguished themselves by their zealousness for God. So having Levi confiscate your property as an Israelite and turn it over to the Imperial Romans would be like us watching a man named George Washington proudly pledge allegiance to a foreign dictatorship from the front steps of the United States Capitol.

Matthew had enemies. Not surprisingly, he was largely excluded from Israelite society. Matthew's closest friends were other tax collectors and those regarded as "sinners" (Luke 5:29–30). He was an outcast, a man without a country even while living in his own home.

Ironically, it is precisely this rejection that made Matthew such a keen observer and commentator on the life of Jesus. As an official in the employ of the Romans, Matthew understood the ways of the world. He was also well trained in the faith, laws, and traditions of his Hebrew ancestors. With a foot firmly planted in each of two very different cultures, Matthew could see the faults and hypocrisies of his own countrymen better than even they could. Matthew was uniquely qualified to tell about the life of Jesus from the perspective of someone who knew what it was like to be an outcast and could smell hypocrisy from a mile away.

Matthew begins his narrative by describing Jesus's royal ancestry. He wanted to remind everyone that Jesus was a descendant of King David. Jesus could not be dismissed as an unsophisticated hillbilly from Galilee. The fact that Israel's political and religious leaders would insult Jesus was further evidence, in Matthew's mind, that they were unreasonable, biased, and close-minded.

Matthew also spends a good deal of time pointing out the

importance of other sinners in Jesus's family tree. Four women are specifically mentioned by Matthew, which is itself unusual in such a male-dominated era, and all of them have a "story." Tamar engaged in prostitution and incest. Rahab was a prostitute. Ruth was a woman from the pagan nation of Moab. Bathsheba became the Queen of Israel only after having an adulterous affair that led to the murder of her devoted husband. Matthew likely includes these individuals in Jesus's family tree because he personally understood the humiliation and isolation these women would have felt. He also knew better than most people that God cares about everyone, regardless of what we have done.

Matthew's Gospel includes the most recorded words of Jesus, thereby providing us with the most expansive collection of his teachings. Matthew also devotes the most attention to connecting the events of Jesus's ministry with the prophecies that foretold of his coming. He particularly relished the fact that Jesus respected the ways of the Israelites without giving in to the peer pressure of religious leaders who had corrupted the Israelites' worship practices.

There are so many intriguing facts about Matthew's life, attitudes, and motivations that we do not know, yet of one thing we may be certain. The future apostle eagerly obeyed when Jesus invited the tax collector to leave his tax booth. Unlike fishermen who could always return to their nets, Matthew gave up a lucrative position to which it would likely be impossible to return. Matthew would never have risked so much if he was not convinced that Jesus was the Christ. We begin to understand just how much God loves everyone by seeing Jesus's ministry through the eyes of one of Israel's biggest outcasts.

Mark

The Gospel of Mark is written from a very different perspective. Although Mark (also known as John Mark) traveled with Paul and Barnabas (Acts 12:25; Acts 13:5; Col. 4:10), he also worked with Luke

(Philem. 24) and Timothy (2 Tim. 4:11). Mark is also frequently associated with the apostle Peter (1 Peter 5:13). In fact, the Gospel of Mark reads very much like the life of Jesus, as witnessed by Peter. This is suggested, in part, by the fact that Mark omits any details of Jesus's ancestry or birth. The book simply starts with Jesus's baptism in the Jordan River, his temptation in the wilderness, and the calling of his first two disciples—Peter and his brother Andrew. The book ends just as abruptly.

Peter's impetuous nature is on display in many of the stories in Mark's Gospel. Jesus had twelve disciples who were closest to him during his earthly ministry. Of these, however, only three were allowed to witness Jesus's transfiguration and go farther into the garden of Gethsemane with Jesus on the night of his arrest. Peter was one of the three.

Peter was the first apostle to publicly state that Jesus was the Christ and son of God, but he was also the apostle who specifically denied Jesus on the night of his arrest. Peter was the only person to join Jesus in a midnight stroll across the maddening waves of the Sea of Galilee in the midst of a raging storm. Throughout Mark's Gospel, Peter is abrasive, stubborn, and prideful, but he is also humble, loyal, and brave. The vast range of Peter's attitudes, emotions, words, and actions demonstrate how similar he was to each of us in many ways.

Mark's Gospel captures the life of Jesus from the perspective of a man who left his fishing nets on the shore to take the chance of a lifetime to follow a young teacher who challenged him to fish for the souls of the lost and oppressed. In time, Peter learns that this calling extends not only to his countrymen but to everyone.

The portrait of Jesus that emerges from Mark is very human, very practical, and very true to life. It is the story of Jesus as experienced by a working man whose three-year journey with Christ set him on a course in life that far surpassed anything he might have dreamed of before. In Mark, we enjoy the perspective of the individual who had the premier front row seat for events as significant as the miracles, the transfiguration, the Last Supper, the empty tomb, and the encounters with Christ that followed.

Luke

The details missing in the Gospel of Mark are often accounted for in the Gospel of Luke. A physician by training (Col. 4:14), Luke used his professional skills of observation and note-taking to produce a two-volume account of the life of Jesus (Luke) and the work of the Holy Spirit in the lives of Jesus's earliest followers (Acts). From the beginning, Luke makes it very clear that he intended to write an "orderly account" of "the things that have been fulfilled among us" (Luke 1:1, 3). Moreover, Luke's Gospel is based upon original sources and accounts of "those who from the first were eyewitnesses and servants of the word" (Luke 1:2). Luke's purpose for undertaking this careful investigation was to give the reader great confidence that the stories about Jesus were genuine and true. Luke tells us, "you may know the certainty of the things you have been taught" (Luke 1:4).

Luke is closely associated with the apostle Paul as they traveled together on several mission journeys (Acts 16–17, 20–21, 27–28). The Gospel of Luke also omits many of the references to the Old Testament and descriptions of Israelite customs found in the other Gospels, which is what we would expect from a Macedonian Gentile such as Luke. While Matthew is written for a predominately Hebrew audience, the book of Luke was likely written primarily with Gentiles in mind.

The physician's understanding of the depth and range of human emotions is also evident in Luke, which emphasizes Jesus's constant concern for those who were mistreated in society, especially women and the poor. Luke provides the fullest account of Jesus's birth. The unique perspective of Mary, Jesus's mother, is captured in both poetry and prose.

The word "joy" appears in the book of Luke almost as frequently as in the other three Gospels combined. Of the three people whom Jesus raised from the dead, only Luke recounts the miracle performed for the benefit of the widow of Nain (Luke 7:11–17). In that passage we see Jesus literally halt a funeral procession as "his heart went out" to the grieving widow, who has also now lost her son, and he tells her, "Don't cry." What is most amazing about this miracle is that the widow did not even ask Jesus to restore her son to life. Jesus performed the greatest miracle imaginable simply because he shared the widow's grief, and he alone had the power to turn her sorrow into joy.

The portrait of Jesus that emerges in Luke is that of a man who suffers and rejoices every bit as much as we do. He is compassionate, purposeful, and eager to serve others. He meets people's immediate needs even while rescuing them from the eternal consequences of sin.

John

If Luke's purpose was to demonstrate that Jesus was human, John's goal was to demonstrate that Jesus was God. John begins with a passage that echoes the first words of Genesis, "In the beginning" (John 1:1). The Gospel of John serves as the prequel to the story of Jesus's eternal existence as described in the book of Revelation. John thereby gives us the most sweeping and inclusive description of Jesus—from his role in creation, through the pivotal events of his earthly ministry, to his eternal kingdom.

John shines a spotlight on Jesus's miracles to prove that his claim to be God is true. Jesus is constantly demonstrating authority over nature, illness, and death—from the first miracle at the wedding in Cana (John 2:1–11) through the miraculous catch of fish following the resurrection (John 21:1–6). Even then, not all of Jesus's miracles are recorded (John 20:30–31; John 21:25). There are simply too many of them.

John's objective in writing his Gospel was to inform subsequent generations of the significance of the fact that God chose to become a human. John demonstrates "that Jesus is the Christ, the son of God" (John 20:31). His account is highly credible because he, along with Peter, was one of the three apostles who were present at the most momentous events in Jesus's ministry.

Nearly half of John's Gospel is dedicated to describing the eight days beginning when Jesus entered Jerusalem in a triumphant procession and ending on the day when he appeared to his disciples after his resurrection. A full quarter of John is focused upon the events that transpired in the upper room during the Last Supper. In the final moments of that gathering (John 17), John records Jesus's prayer for himself, his disciples, and all believers in all generations that would follow. The Gospel of John is not just about Jesus's interactions with people he encountered—it tells the grand story of Jesus's concern for everyone.

Reflection

Each of the Gospels inspires us to grow closer to Jesus. Taken together, however, they provide a collection of teachings and examples that are too fundamental to deny, too essential to ignore, and too important to forget. The four Gospels are a quartet of calling birds that tell one amazing story.

By focusing upon our relationship with Jesus on the fourth day of Christmas, our true love is inviting us to experience God's good news in a way that we can understand and appreciate. Our true love helps us see Jesus through the eyes of those who knew him best in order that we may know him better.

Entering into a meaningful, long-term relationship is difficult, however. Everyone has been burned at least once, and having a relationship soured during Christmas is especially traumatic. Our true love knows this, of course. He will not force himself upon us. We are free to stop celebrating Christmas any time we want.

Still, the thought of having eight more gifts to open is exciting. We can be certain that those gifts will further assure us that accepting the invitation to grow in our relationship with Jesus will be worthwhile and beneficial. Over the next two days, our true love will give us gifts that reveal the extent of God's faithfulness and power. What comes next is the proof that the Gospels' promises are true and that the invitation to know Christ is genuine.

December 29

Five Golden Rings
The Pentateuch – God Keeps
His Promises

On the fifth day of Christmas, my true love gave to me ...
Five golden rings,
Four calling birds, three French hens,
Two turtledoves, and a partridge in a pear tree.

It is time to start getting serious about our New Year's resolutions. Will we resolve to lose the weight we gained between Thanksgiving and Christmas? Will we resolve to spend less money, or will we resolve to restore a broken relationship? Here is my favorite: will we resolve not to make any resolutions? When the fifth day of Christmas rolls around, our newest promises to ourselves are starting to take shape.

Promises are the focus of our true love's fifth gift. Yesterday's gift invited us to develop a closer, personal relationship with Jesus Christ. Accepting the invitation requires a major commitment on our part, however. We may hesitate to throw ourselves headlong into such a relationship if there are no promises to back it up. Some assurances are necessary. That is what makes today's gift so perfect.

After giving us an aviary full of birds, our true love finally gives us something that is obviously valuable: five golden rings. The gift immediately reminds us of the most enduring tradition of a wedding ceremony, when the bride and groom exchange rings while making promises to one another. The wedding ring's precious metal reminds us of the tremendous value placed upon the institution of marriage. Likewise, the ring's circular shape indicates that a loving commitment never stops. Both of these ideas are present in today's gift.

But wait, there's more.

Instead of giving us just one ring, our true love gives us no less than five bright, shiny, glistening, beautiful golden rings. The number of rings adds a second layer of symbolism to our true love's gift. In addition to reminding us of God's loving and eternal promise to Christians, the five rings also remind us of God's past promise to the nation of Israel. The story of God making and keeping that promise is told in the Pentateuch, which is the name given to the first five books of the Old Testament. Since God kept his promise to Israel, we can be confident he will also keep his promise to us when we accept Jesus as our Lord and Savior.

Genesis

Genesis begins with the memorable words, "In the beginning, God created." Even before there was a concept of time, God existed. That, in and of itself, is a concept too fantastic to fully comprehend.

Genesis describes the creation, which climaxes with God forming Adam and Eve and placing them in the Garden of Eden. The utopia is destroyed, however, when they disobey God. Adam and Eve's sin means they are no longer able to live in God's direct presence. They are forced to work hard to survive. They will one day die.

As the story continues, all seems lost. God "grieve[s] that he had made man on the earth and his heart was filled with pain" (Gen. 6:6). He makes the heartbreaking decision to start over. Though sin cannot be undone, its consequences may be reset. To accomplish this, God counts on Noah, the one man who remained faithful. Noah builds an ark and takes animals into it before God's judgment falls upon the earth. After spending over a year in the ark, Noah, his family, and the animals are able to step foot on dry land once again.

Unfortunately, the memory of the flood is insufficient to prevent Noah's family from sinning once more. As they repopulate the world, their sins go with them. God confuses their language and scatters them across the earth in order to delay the need for another judgment. Nevertheless, generation after generation rejects him.

So God does something different. Instead of trying to work with everyone, he reveals himself to one man in particular. God counts on the fact that when he is able to demonstrate his love, mercy, and kindness to one man and his family, the example will be so compelling that everyone will desire the same relationship. This man, Abram, leaves his home and finally makes his way to the land where God leads him. Abram builds three altars to worship God, with each altar being a reminder of God's promise to give this vast land to Abram's descendants. God's promise seems ridiculous, however. Abram and his wife are well beyond the childbearing years, and they have no children.

Abram's faith is sincere, but it is not perfect. He tries to "help" God fulfill his promise, but Abram's efforts are counterproductive. Each time Abram relies upon himself, he ends up making the fulfillment of God's promise more difficult.

The most crucial moment in Abram's life is recorded in Genesis 17. It has been twenty-four years since he obeyed God's command to leave his homeland. He still does not have a son with his wife. Abram is discouraged. How can God possibly keep his promise to give him many descendants with a homeland of their own? The answer comes when God reveals himself to Abram and tells him:

> As for me, this is my covenant with you. You will
> be the father of many nations. No longer will you

be called Abram; your name will be Abraham,
for I have made you a father of many nations. I
will make you very fruitful; I will make nations of
you, and kings will come from you. I will establish
my covenant as an everlasting covenant between
me and you and your descendants after you for
the generations to come, to be your God and the
God of your descendants after you. The whole
land of Canaan, where you are now an alien, I will
give as an everlasting possession to you and your
descendants after you, and I will be their God.
(Gen. 17:4–8)

And then Abraham and Sarah miraculously have a son whom
they name Isaac. God shares his promise to Abraham with Isaac,
but it still seems so far-fetched. Isaac's twin sons, Jacob and Esau,
do not get along well at all. Jacob manipulates Esau to steal his
brother's birthright and then, with the help of his mother, tricks
Isaac into giving the family blessing to him instead of Esau. Esau
threatens to kill his deceitful brother.

Jacob runs away and spends twenty years living in the household
of his uncle, Laban. Ironically, Laban is even more treacherous than
Jacob. Jacob is tricked into marrying Laban's oldest daughter, Leah,
before being allowed to marry the woman he loves, Laban's younger
daughter, Rachel. God blesses Jacob during this period of exile, which
makes Laban intensely jealous. Again, Jacob is forced to run away.
His anxiety is very high as he is pursued by his father-in-law while
traveling along the road that will return him to his brother, Esau.

Jacob's fears are misplaced. After showing Jacob the foolishness
of his deceitful ways, God renames him Israel.

Though Jacob finds peace with his extended family, his own
household is a case study in dysfunction. Jacob loves Rachel but is
cruel to Leah. However, Rachel is barren while Leah has several
sons. Rachel retaliates by making her servant become a surrogate

mother. Leah responds by forcing her own servant to also serve as a surrogate mother when she is temporarily unable to have children. Finally, Rachel is able to have children, but then dies while giving birth to her second son. Rachel's sons quickly become Jacob's favorites, to the disgust of their ten older brothers.

Genesis concludes with Joseph, Rachel's oldest son, being sold into slavery by his brothers. Through an unexpected turn of events, Joseph becomes the second most powerful man in Egypt. He then understands that his enslavement was always part of God's plan to fulfill the promise to Abraham, Isaac, and Jacob. Joseph uses his power to supply the food necessary to sustain his family during a famine lasting seven years.

At Joseph's urging, Jacob's entire household moves to Egypt. Jacob's dying request, however, is to be buried in the land of Abraham and Isaac. Joseph persuades Pharaoh to allow this to happen and Genesis ends with Joseph making his own final request to be buried with his forefathers.

Exodus

The fulfillment of God's promise to Abraham continues in Exodus. Joseph's achievements are forgotten by the Egyptian leaders who despise Jacob's descendants (now called Israelites). They fiercely oppress the Israelites and slaughter their male infants. One Israelite mother hides her baby son in a small basket that she sets in the Nile River. The child is found by Pharaoh's daughter, perhaps by design. The princess adopts the child and names him Moses.

Moses becomes an influential leader, but is forced to flee Egypt when it is discovered that he killed an Egyptian who was mistreating an Israelite slave. Moses is forty years old when he leaves Egypt and he spends the next forty years living a humble existence as a shepherd in the wastelands.

Everything changes one day when Moses comes upon a bush that is on fire but is not consumed by the flames. In this encounter with God, Moses makes every excuse he can think of to avoid the task set before him, but ultimately he obeys. Moses sets out to free the Israelites from Egyptian bondage and bring them back to the land first promised to Abraham. Pharaoh is stubborn. Moses is frustrated. God is faithful.

Pharaoh finally allows the Israelites to leave after ten plagues devastate Egypt. Passover, the day when the final plague results in the death of the firstborn male in every Egyptian household, becomes the most important day on Israel's calendar, annually reminding them of God's faithfulness to his promises. The events of the first portion of Exodus are epic in every sense of the word.

What follows is more important, however. At Mount Sinai, God formally includes the entire nation of Israel as the beneficiaries of his promise to Abraham. Though four hundred years have passed since God first spoke to Abraham, the promise is still alive. God is faithful!

All is well until the people grow restless and press Moses's brother, Aaron, to construct a golden calf to worship as an idol. In the midst of their rowdy party, Moses returns to the camp and angrily smashes the law tablets given by God. Thousands of Israelites die as a punishment for their rebellion against God.

The promise is saved, however, when Moses asks God to forgive the Israelites. Once again, the promise given to Abraham, Isaac, Jacob, and the Israelites is renewed. Exodus concludes with the Israelites embracing the promise by contributing the materials necessary to construct a tabernacle to be a physical reminder of God's presence in their camp. In the final scene in Exodus, God's glory fills the tabernacle.

Leviticus

The events of Leviticus all take place during the eleven months that Israel camps at Mount Sinai. The Israelites are given precise rules on who may approach God's presence (the priests) and what they are to do when they get there (rituals and sacrifices). The rest of Leviticus explains the sacrifices and holy seasons Israel is to observe as well as the practical rules necessary for keeping the people healthy while living in a rustic camp.

Leviticus is considered one of the least interesting books of the Bible because it contains so many rules. Certainly, the pace of the drama that unfolds across the pages of Genesis and Exodus slows down significantly in Leviticus, and many who resolve to read the entire Bible in one year find their goal slipping away somewhere in the passages on ritual sacrifice and priestly garments.

Diminishing the significance of this book is a major mistake, however. Leviticus is the basis for the relationship between God and Israel that prevailed for over one thousand years and, more importantly, the rules of Leviticus still applied to Israel during the time of Jesus's ministry. To get the most out of the Gospels, it is helpful to have a basic understanding of the pattern of Israelite life established in Leviticus.

Without Leviticus, how would we know that God's promise to us as Christians is better than the promise he made to Abraham and his descendants? As the author of Hebrews writes, this new covenant "is superior to the old one, since [it] is established on better promises" (Heb. 8:12). Those promises include having eternal life in God's presence and our sins being forgiven and remembered no more. Thus, Leviticus formalizes the promise between God and Israel and sets the stage for the even greater promise that God would later establish with us through Jesus. Leviticus no longer applies to our daily lives, but it helps us understand and appreciate the privileged relationship we have with God.

Numbers

With a renewed covenant, a national identity, and a firm understanding of God's expectations, the Israelites set off to possess the land promised to Abraham. However, ten of Moses's twelve spies report that any military campaign will be doomed to fail. The Israelites panic and refuse to go any farther, even when God promises them victories.

God's anger is so great that he threatens to destroy Israel and restart the effort to fulfill the promise to Abraham through the children of Moses. Moses once again pleads on behalf of the Israelites. God responds with mercy.

Nevertheless, as punishment, the Israelites will be given the very thing they want. Instead of marching into the Promised Land, they will return to the wilderness for forty years to live as a homeless nation. A journey that was intended to last only a few months is extended by an entire generation.

At the end of that period, God once again leads Israel toward the Promised Land. A new generation of Israelites gain land and position themselves along the plains east of the Jordan River. Numbers concludes with the Israelites ready to move forward at God's command.

Deuteronomy

While Leviticus sets the stage for Jesus's ministry, Deuteronomy is the book that Jesus quotes most frequently. Jesus refers to Deuteronomy 6:4–5 as the greatest commandment: "Hear, O Israel: The LORD our God, the LORD is one. Love the LORD your God with all your heart and with all your soul and with all your strength." This declaration kindles a fire of devotion to God that is never extinguished throughout the rest of the Bible. Paul expresses the essence of this command by later writing, "Therefore, I urge you brothers and sisters, in view of God's mercy, to offer your bodies as a living sacrifice—holy and pleasing to God—this is your true and proper worship" (Rom. 12:1).

Deuteronomy also provides the framework for understanding how Israel fits into God's ultimate plan. In keeping his promise to Abraham, God is also moving forward with his even greater plan to save all nations from the curses of sin. The Israelites will receive a homeland, but they will also share in the heritage of blessing all people by being the nation from which the Christ will come. By continuing in a tradition of faith established by their ancestor Abraham, the Israelites become a witness to other nations of the power, goodness, mercy, love, and faithfulness of God.

Reflection

Promises are hard to keep, even when we make them to ourselves. So when we think about making a permanent commitment to have a personal relationship with Jesus, the question of whether he will be a faithful partner and a genuine friend naturally crosses our mind. Our true love's gift of five golden rings symbolizes that God's promise is precious, eternal, and magnificent. The gift also reminds us that God has an excellent track record for keeping his promises.

Like an old friend who knows us better than we know ourselves, our true love's generosity continues to touch our hearts. His gifts are responding to our greatest needs and bringing peace to our souls.

Though we may already be past the point when we say, "Yes! I want Jesus!" Christmas is not even half over. Our true love has seven more gifts to give, and he is not content to show himself to be just a little generous. He desires to be the definition of generosity. Tomorrow's gift will demonstrate the awesome, mind-blowing extent of God's power. Not only does God keep his promises, he can do anything.

December 30

Six Geese a Laying
The Creation – God's Power is Immeasurable

On the sixth day of Christmas, my true love gave to me …
Six geese a laying,
Five golden rings,
Four calling birds, three French hens,
Two turtledoves, and a partridge in a pear tree.

The sixth day of Christmas is filled with anticipation as we prepare to usher in a brand new year just one day after tomorrow. By now, any remaining Christmas items are piled up on the clearance shelves. The prime retail space is dedicated to Winter White Sale goods and Valentine's Day merchandise. You may also notice that department store mannequins are starting to showcase the early colors of spring. Car lots across the nation are filled with salesmen desperately trying to satisfy sales quotas.

Our true love has something new in mind today as well. The gift of six plump geese that are laying their eggs provides a vivid image of new life. Though winter is only nine days old, here is another reminder that spring is just around the corner.

But before we can fully appreciate the significance of today's gift, it is important to see how it relates to our last two gifts. We now know that the four calling birds symbolize the Gospels and invite us into a meaningful relationship with Jesus. Likewise, the five golden rings symbolically remind us of the promise God makes to those who accept this invitation as well as the fact that God's record for keeping his promises is perfect.

Today's gift offers us further assurance that God's invitation is real. We do not have to decide whether to follow Jesus based solely upon the Gospel stories or how God previously interacted with the nation of Israel. Our true love's sixth gift confirms that God has the power to keep his promise to us. His power is so great that even a measuring stick the size of the universe would not be big enough to fully describe what God can do.

So how do six laboring geese symbolize God's awesome power? The six geese remind us of the creation account set forth in Genesis 1–2. In six remarkable days, God created the heavens, the earth and all that is in them. Today, God's awesome power to create is represented by our true love's gift of six geese bringing forth their own new creation. By reminding us of God's ultimate power and authority, our true love is telling us that the invitation to follow Jesus is backed by immeasurable power.

Learning About God through Creation

The creation account in Genesis is God's way of introducing himself to humanity. We discover God's personality as he shares his opinion throughout the six days of creation. While God describes most of what he has created as "good," the only thing that he describes as "very good" is the one thing that he makes in his own image—humans (Gen. 1:31). Our "very goodness" is also evident in the fact that only humans are "formed" by God and given "the breath of life" (Gen. 2:7, 22).

The creation account in Genesis 1 demonstrates that God's actions are thoughtful and deliberate. In the first three days of creation, God's efforts are focused upon the basics: creating matter and light, making the heavens and the earth, dividing the waters of the earth into the sky and surface waters and then separating the waters by the emergence of land and vegetation. God populates these environments in the same order during the final three days of creation: the sun, moon and stars fill the heavens, birds and fish populate the skies and waters, animals appear on the land, and, finally, a man and a woman are placed in the Garden of Eden. The simplicity and order in which God's creative acts are described in Genesis testifies to his intelligence, artistry, and attention to detail.

God also uses creation to illustrate his spiritual qualities. For instance, on the first day of creation, God speaks light into existence. The displacement of darkness by light becomes the perfect metaphor for God's involvement in people's lives right up through our own time. In John's Gospel, Jesus tells the people, "I am the light of the world. Whoever follows me will never walk in darkness, but will have the light of life" (John 8:12). During the Sermon on the Mount, Jesus extends the analogy to his disciples when he describes them as "the light of the world" (Matt. 5:14). By accepting the invitation to follow Jesus, we share in this rich heritage of ridding the world of darkness by reflecting God's character.

Acknowledging God's Power

Although the creation account is meant to serve as an introduction to God, it has regrettably become a source of controversy in modern times. Many are simply unwilling to embrace Genesis 1–2 as factual. Regardless of our understanding of the universe's origins, one fact is undeniable: every account, theory, and description of creation must be based upon something other than personal observation because no one was physically present to witness the creation. Nor do we have the ability to look back in time to the original condition of the universe. Thus, every theory of creation ultimately requires some exercise of faith. In terms of deciding whether we will acknowledge God's power on the sixth day of Christmas, the real question before us is not whether faith is required to accept the Genesis account (or any other explanation of the universe's origin), but rather how much faith is required to accept it.

The Great Puzzle

I am always excited to see how advances in science are allowing us to discover the previously hidden structures and processes of creation. The Hubble Telescope gives us awe-inspiring images of distant nebulas. Advanced microscopes reveal the elegant simplicity of DNA's replicating double helix. We see the amazing sophistication that was previously unknown as we perceive creation in increasingly greater levels of detail.

The intricacies and interactions of nature are all equally well described by scientists, theologians, poets, and artists. Nobel Prize–winning physicist Frank Wilczek describes the elegance of the universe this way: "There is great beauty and simplicity here, but it is only fully evident when we understand the deep design." Some would dismiss the exquisite nature of the universe as the result of time and chance, but the obvious explanation is that creation is covered with God's fingerprints and testifies to his existence.

As Paul writes in Romans 1:20, "For since the creation of the world God's invisible qualities—his eternal power and divine nature—have been clearly seen, being understood from what has been made, so that men are without excuse." This passage challenges us to explore the mysteries of the universe. In Jeremiah 33:2, God says, "This is what the LORD, says, he who made the earth, the LORD who formed it and established it—the LORD is his name: 'Call to me and I will answer you and tell you great and unsearchable things you do not know.'"

The notion that the quarks, electrons, and neutrinos of a single atom and a black hole's singularity are part of a great cosmic puzzle just waiting to be pieced together is intellectually thrilling.

It inspires us to ask questions, test theories, and build knowledge. God does not fear our curiosity. He welcomes it. The desire to know and understand ourselves and our environment is one of the fundamental characteristics that make us "very good" in God's eyes.

Historical Credibility

The creation events remind us that we will always be one big family, regardless of how hard we try to divide ourselves by race, gender, politics, nationality, economic status, or other characteristics. The common history shared by all humans helps explain why creation is the single most recognized tale of all time. Virtually every tribe, culture, and ethnic group has a creation story in its heritage. While the details vary, there are common elements to most all of these stories.

So why should we accept Genesis's account of creation as being more credible than other accounts?

It is widely accepted that Moses was the author of the Pentateuch—Genesis, Exodus, Leviticus, Numbers, and Deuteronomy. We often forget, however, that Moses claimed to speak directly with God during many key points in his life. Moses's "source" for the creation account was none other than the Creator himself.

While some may be tempted to dismiss Moses's claims as foolish embellishments, the implications of such a decision are greater than we might think. For instance, Moses also claimed that the Ten Commandments were divinely inspired. This puts the account of creation in Genesis 1–2 on an equal historical footing with the recitation of the Ten Commandments in Exodus 20.

If we accept that the Ten Commandments are authentic, we have no less reason to accept Moses's account of creation as well. In fact, the fourth of the Ten Commandments is directly associated with the Genesis creation account. In Exodus 20:8–11, the Israelites are told to keep the Sabbath (the seventh day of the week) holy as a reminder that God created the heavens and the earth in six days before resting on the seventh day.

Billions of people of differing faiths accept the historical account of Abraham, as recorded by Moses, even though Abraham predated Moses by about four centuries. It would be difficult to say Moses accurately described Abraham's life but imagined the whole creation account. There is simply no intellectual basis to think that Moses was the faithful, divinely inspired scribe for most portions of Genesis through Deuteronomy and a fiction novelist for the balance of those books. The first five books of the Bible must be read as one consistent, true story.

The Testimony of Others

Finally, it comes as no surprise that God's status as the Creator of the universe becomes a familiar reference for later Biblical authors. In Isaiah 44:24, the prophet delivers this message: "This is what the LORD says—your Redeemer, who formed you in the womb: I am the LORD, who has made all things, who alone stretched out the heavens, who spread out the earth by myself." In the next chapter, Isaiah uses the creation story to demonstrate that there is only one God when he writes in Isaiah 45:18, "For this is what the LORD says—he who created the heavens, he is God; he who fashioned and made the earth, he founded it; he did not create it to be empty, but formed it to be inhabited—he says: 'I am the LORD, and there is no other.'"

In Psalm 19:1–4, David speaks to the manner in which creation testifies of God's glory to all people in all places at all times, when he writes:

> The heavens declare the glory of God; the skies
> proclaim the work of his hands. Day after day they
> pour fourth speech; night after night they display

knowledge. There is no speech or language where
their voice is not heard. Their voice goes out into
all the earth, their words to the ends of the world.

Hezekiah also acknowledges God's power (2 Kings 19:15), as
does Jeremiah, a prophet who prays, "Ah, Sovereign LORD, you
have made the heavens and the earth by your great power and
outstretched arm. Nothing is too hard for you" (Jer. 32:17).

While it may not be surprising that these and other faithful
Israelites professed their belief in God as the Creator, the Bible
includes several examples of non-Israelites who also shared this
belief. Melchizedek, the king and priest of Salem, gave this blessing
to Abram: "Blessed be Abram by God Most High, Creator of heaven
and earth" (Gen. 14:19). Likewise, Hiram, the king of Tyre, praised
God by writing, "Praise be to the LORD, the God of Israel, who
made heaven and earth!" (2 Chron. 2:12).

In the New Testament, Jesus and others carry forward the
central theme of Genesis 1–2 that God is the all-powerful Creator
of the universe. Paul describes God in Acts 14:15 as "the living God,
who made heaven and earth and sea and everything in them." Peter
echoes the point in his second letter when he states, "long ago by
God's word the heavens existed and the earth was formed" (2 Peter
3:5). In Hebrews 11:3, a person's faith is measured in part by the
acceptance of God as the Creator: "By faith we understand that the
universe was formed at God's command, so that what is seen was
not made out of what was visible."

Reflection

What we believe about creation significantly shapes what we
believe about God. If we think that the Genesis account of creation
is nothing more than a myth or ancient fable, there is a good chance
that God's own character and nature will seem less personal and
more distant. On the other hand, when we accept the creation

account in Genesis as true and authentic, we acknowledge God's power, his plan for creating the universe, and, ultimately, his concern for each of us.

As with all things, what we believe is left for us to decide. The creation story is offered by our true love as proof that God is powerful enough to do anything, including keeping his promises to us.

Today also represents the midpoint of the Christmas season. Starting with the most important gift on the very first day of Christmas, our true love has now given us six gifts that successively draw us closer to Jesus. Now, perhaps for the first time, a question arises in our minds.

Why?

Why would God desire to know me personally and why does he value a close relationship with me? Why is the God who knows the name of one hundred trillion stars also concerned with how I treated my spouse, my child, my friend, my neighbor, or my colleague today? Why does he care what I plan to do tomorrow?

These questions are legitimate and must be answered if our relationship with Jesus is to be real and have purpose and meaning. And yet, as we might have guessed, our true love is still one step ahead of us. God's concern for us, and his perfect intention for our well-being, will continue to manifest itself in our true love's next six gifts.

December 31

Seven Swans a Swimming
The Holy Spirit's Gifts – Help
for God's People

On the seventh day of Christmas, my true love gave to me ...
Seven swans a swimming,
Six geese a laying,
Five golden rings,
Four calling birds, three French hens,
Two turtledoves, and a partridge in a pear tree.

Today is one long countdown. As the final day of the year, we cannot help glancing at the clock a little more frequently. New Year's Eve differs from Christmas in one very significant respect. Christmas is celebrated only by Christians, but the arrival of the New Year is a global event. Images from Sydney and Singapore and Moscow and London all precede the most famous New Year's Eve ritual of them all—the dropping of the crystal ball in Times Square. We all have our New Year's Eve traditions, whether it is staying up well into the morning, going to bed early, or simply falling asleep just a few minutes short of midnight.

Yet midnight comes and goes so quickly that not even a camera can capture the moment and preserve it perfectly. The future and history are always nanoseconds apart, but we never know what will happen just a few minutes from now, nor can we ever change what has just occurred. The passage of time is mysterious.

Our true love's seventh gift is also mysterious. His seven swimming swans are symbolic of what happens when we accept the invitation to build a relationship with Jesus and allow the Holy Spirit to guide our lives. Our true love's seventh gift perfectly illustrates the benefits that come from following Jesus.

We need look no further than Hans Christian Anderson's classic story, "The Ugly Duckling," to understand this symbolism. As we recall, a baby swan is called a cygnet. Cygnets are awkward and unattractive. As time passes, however, a cygnet matures and becomes the very picture of beauty and grace. The swan is even a symbol of royalty in some countries. Today's gift of a mature swan vividly illustrates the process of spiritual growth that is made possible through the Holy Spirit.

Our true love is giving us seven swans, however, not just one. The number seven is associated with perfection and completeness in the Bible, so today's gift is also symbolic of a perfect and complete growth process. Such a result is only possible in a spiritual sense when our lifestyle resembles the way that Jesus lived his life. Again, it is the Holy Spirit who helps us act like Jesus by continuously revealing God's nature in each of our lives.

At this point in the Christmas season, we are growing accustomed to the multiple layers of symbolism attached to each of our true love's gifts. It is perhaps unsurprising to learn that there is a third element of symbolism in today's gift as well. In addition to being symbolic of maturity and acting like Christ, the seven swans also remind us of the seven unique skills the Holy Spirit gives to Christians. These skills aid our spiritual growth and enrich our relationships with other Christians. Thus, the perfect and complete maturity that results from the Holy Spirit's spiritual gifts is our true love's real gift on this seventh day of Christmas.

The Holy Spirit

Properly understanding the Holy Spirit is a challenge for many Christians. We understand that our Heavenly Father and Jesus are one and the same, but the Holy Spirit is also an equal part of God. Without a doubt, the Holy Spirit is the least understood and most mysterious part of the Trinity.

The Holy Spirit as Part of the Trinity of God

The notion that God could exist in three separate but unified ways is hard to understand. Nevertheless, we know that God exists as the Father, as Jesus, and as the Holy Spirit—all at the same time. Children's author Joanne Marxhausen uses an apple to explain this concept. As an apple has three elements (the outer skin, pulp, and seeds), God exists as the Father, the Son, and the Holy Spirit. Three separate elements may all comprise one complete thing.

While we see the three aspects of God at work in different ways in the Bible, there is no single passage that completely describes his role as our Father, as Jesus, and as the Holy Spirit. Instead, we are left with a tapestry of scriptures that offer a picture of God that is both pleasingly simple and somewhat mysterious. The one thing of which we may be certain is that God has intentionally chosen to reveal himself to us in different ways at different times for different purposes.

The Holy Spirit as "Another Helper"

Jesus described the Holy Spirit to his followers as "another helper" (John 14:15–27). They did not truly understand what he meant, however, until the Holy Spirit empowered them to miraculously speak in foreign languages at Pentecost (Acts 2). By personally experiencing the Holy Spirit, these men performed miracles and boldly proclaimed the Gospel.

The Holy Spirit works with us when we have a relationship

with Jesus. The Holy Spirit is so vital to our spiritual growth that he actually dwells within us (John 7:38; Rom. 8:9–11). He removes the burdens of guilt and sorrow we bear (2 Cor. 5:17; Titus 3:5–6), and helps us develop a deeper knowledge and understanding of Jesus (2 Peter 3:18). This makes it easier to serve God and others (Rom. 4:12; Rom. 8:14; Gal. 5:16–18; Eph. 5:18). Without the Holy Spirit, it would be impossible to grow and mature as Christians.

The Holy Spirit's Work

The Holy Spirit's work in our lives is a beautiful thing, but how much more fantastic is it to see the Holy Spirit working simultaneously in the lives of many Christians, all for their mutual benefit? This is the aspect of the Holy Spirit's work that is at the forefront of our true love's mind today. While other passages describe additional spiritual gifts, Romans 12:6–8 lists seven spiritual skills that are inspired by the Holy Spirit.

The Gift of Prophecy

The gift of prophecy was given to some of Jesus Christ's earliest believers in order to facilitate the rapid spread of the gospel. Before the New Testament was written, before the apostles traveled across three continents, and before the early church enjoyed basic freedoms to assemble and worship, Christians with a prophetic gift were divinely inspired to deliver a specific message from God when such a message was needed (Acts 21:10–11).

As the church grew, the need for believers to speak prophetically diminished. Questions of faith are now answered by consulting the New Testament. No additional information is required to have a friendship with Jesus, because God has revealed himself to us.

Nevertheless, we cannot say with certainty that the gift of prophecy is extinguished altogether. Though Paul indicates the gift of prophecy would one day cease (1 Cor. 13:8), there are still people who have never heard the gospel. The Holy Spirit has the ability and authority to speak to whomever he wants, however he wants, whenever he wants, about whatever he wants. The gift of prophecy therefore highlights one of the mysteries that continues to surround the Holy Spirit.

The Gift of Service

Service is associated with meeting the needs of others. James writes that to "look after the interests of orphans and widows in their distress" is both pure and faultless (James 1:27). Paul described offering our bodies in service to others as a "living sacrifice" that is "holy and pleasing to God" and a "spiritual act of worship" (Rom. 12:1).

While we easily agree with these statements, putting them into practice is often more difficult. Serving others is an unnatural act for many of us. We sometimes need the Holy Spirit's help to have the desire to unselfishly serve others.

The Holy Spirit never presents us with opportunities to serve others while at the same time depriving us of the strength necessary to accomplish the task at hand. Peter writes that we "should [serve] with the strength God provides" (1 Peter 4:11). God promises to give us the strength we need to accomplish his will (Phil. 4:13). No matter how overwhelming a situation may seem, we are assured that the Holy Spirit's strength is available to work through us to accomplish God's will.

Equally important, the Holy Spirit demonstrates that we are putting love into action whenever we lend someone a hand. Our service to others is a classic example of *agape*, part of our true love's third gift and the cornerstone of a virtuous, well-lived life. Hebrews 13:6, makes the point clear: "And do not forget to do good and to share with others, for with such sacrifices God is pleased." When our love for God is genuine, serving others becomes a reflection of that love. What might once have been considered a burden is now a great privilege. The Holy Spirit gives us the opportunity to say "thank you" to God by doing something kind for others.

The Gift of Teaching

Teaching is similar to service, but this time we use words, not actions, to share the gospel. We sometimes miss our opportunities to tell others about Jesus because we assume the gospel can only be taught as part of a structured activity in a formal setting, such as a Sunday morning sermon. When we insist on waiting for the perfect moment to share our faith, we are probably missing many good opportunities to describe our relationship with Jesus to others.

Consider this. Paul liked to explain the gospel amidst the chaos of the public market. Indeed, the most common setting for teaching the gospel in the New Testament was in the home when small groups of Christians gathered to share a meal. Teaching often occurs whenever an opportunity arises and wherever the student is most comfortable. Paul says it this way: "Be wise in the way you act towards outsiders; make the most of every opportunity" (Col. 4:5).

It is also wrong to assume we should not teach *anything* about the gospel until we are ready to teach *everything* about the gospel. We forget that when Peter writes, "Always be prepared to give an answer to everyone who asks you to give the reason for the hope that you have" (1 Peter 3:15b), his advice is for us to have "an answer," not to have "all the answers."

Likewise, when Peter writes that we should speak "with gentleness and respect, keeping a clear conscience" (1 Pet. 3:15), he is reminding us that "how we say it" is just as important as "what we say." Many times, creating opportunities to share the gospel is as simple as saying, "God bless you," or asking, "How may I pray for you?"

Finally, we should know that boldness is the Holy Spirit's specialty. In Acts 4, Christians prayed that God would enable them to "speak your word with great boldness." What followed was a period of amazing growth and unity in the church. In Philippians 1:14, Paul writes how his own challenging circumstances emboldened others to "speak the word of God more courageously and fearlessly." Paul wrote to the Colossians, "Pray that I may proclaim [the Gospel] clearly, as I should" (Col. 4:4).

I have never sincerely prayed for boldness to share the gospel and then had to wait for months, or even days, for an opportunity to do so. The bigger problem is that I do not pray that prayer often enough! The Holy Spirit is usually waiting on us.

The Gift of Encouragement

One of the greatest things we can give away is an encouraging word. Encouragement is itself a characteristic of God. In Psalm 10:17–18, David writes, "You hear, O LORD, the desire of the afflicted; you encourage them, and you listen to their cry, defending the fatherless and the oppressed, in order that man, who is of the earth, may terrify no more." We are reflecting God's nature whenever we share a brighter perspective on difficult circumstances or offer empathy for someone in distress.

John Greenleaf Whittier once wrote, "For of all sad words of tongue or pen, the saddest of these: 'It might have been!'" The point of Whittier's poem becomes self-evident as we grow older. Regret is a destructive emotion, robbing us of joy in the present and our hope for the future. The antidote for regret is an encouraging word, administered liberally. The Holy Spirit works through us, as Paul writes in 1 Thessalonians 5:11, to "encourage one another and build each other up."

The Gift of Generosity

Generosity leads us to eagerly give our stuff away. The model for generosity is the Christian believers who lived in Macedonia. In 2 Corinthians 8, Paul writes that, although they were very poor, "out of the most severe trial, their overflowing joy and their extreme poverty welled up in rich generosity" (2 Cor. 8:2). The Macedonians "gave as much as they were able, and even beyond their ability" (2 Cor. 8:3). In fact, they "urgently pleaded … for the privilege of sharing in this service to the saints" (2 Cor. 8:4).

The Macedonians' example personifies the character of the "cheerful giver" (2 Cor. 9:7). Do we consider it a privilege to give money or other property to others? The Holy Spirit challenges us to examine the priority we place upon possessing things instead of sharing them with others.

When we give to others out of a sense of guilt or obligation, we find that our act of giving is unsatisfying or even irritating. We end up limiting the Holy Spirit's ability to work within us, and we are depriving ourselves of the joy that results from taking part in a cause greater than our own selfishness. To be sincere, our generosity must acknowledge God's generosity toward us.

Only then may the Holy Spirit use our generosity to broaden our view of the world by seeing—and meeting—the needs of others.

The Gift of Leadership

We think of a leader as a person who speaks with authority, commands attention, and has significant influence over the lives of many people. Christian leaders have these characteristics, but they result from acting like Jesus and not from imposing their own wishes on others. For instance, in Luke 9:51–56, James and John volunteer to call fire down from heaven in order to punish a Samaritan city for being inhospitable. The brothers were shocked when Jesus scolded them for their "leadership."

Jesus's definition of leadership is radically different. He told his disciples that the one who would be considered the greatest among them would be the one who most humbly devoted himself to the service of others (Mark 10:35–44).

The point echoes throughout the New Testament. Paul writes to Timothy, "Do not let anyone look down on you because you are young, but set an example for the believers in speech, in life, in love, in faith and in purity" (1Tim. 4:12). Similar advice is given to Titus: "In everything set them an example, by doing what is good" (Titus 2:7). A true leader is one whose life resembles the work of Jesus. The leader becomes a model for others to follow.

We know this is true. The people who have the most profound impact in our lives do not have public relations firms on retainer, corner offices, or speechwriters. They are the individuals who invest their time in our well-being and growth. They show us how to find meaning in life and teach us the value of our relationship with God. These are the men and women gifted by the Holy Spirit with leadership. As Paul writes, "Follow my example, as I follow the example of Christ" (1 Cor. 11:1).

The Gift of Mercy

The Holy Spirit's seventh gift is mercy. We love mercy because we need so much of it. We know that we have many sins in our lives (Rom. 3:23) and that these sins separate us from God (1 John 3:4–6). If our relationship to God ended there, it would be a great tragedy.

Thankfully, our story does not end with sin and death. For a week now, we have been daily reminded that Jesus came to earth to be crucified so we might escape the punishment our sins required. Jesus's sacrifice is the perfect example of mercy. It is an act so magnificent and epic that it is forever memorialized in passages such as John 3:16, "For God so loved the world that he gave his one and only son, that whoever believes in him shall not perish but have eternal life."

No one understood the power of mercy better than Paul. Before becoming a great missionary, Paul was best known for his eagerness to kill Christians. It took a miraculous vision of Jesus to show Paul that his life's work was misdirected toward evil. Not a day would have passed that Paul failed to recall the face of each and every Christian he had tortured and killed. Through the Holy Spirit's power, Paul experienced mercy, and it changed his life:

Even thou I was once a blasphemer and a persecutor and a violent man, I was shown mercy … Christ Jesus came into the world to save sinners—of whom I am the worst. But for that very reason I was shown mercy so that in me, the worst of sinners, Christ Jesus might display his unlimited patience as an example for those who would believe in him and receive eternal life.

(1 Tim. 1:13, 15–16)

Reflection

With the current year rapidly drawing to a close, our true love's seventh gift draws our attention to the Holy Spirit's work in bringing us along to perfect maturity in Christ. The Holy Spirit has helped Christians for two thousand years, never ceasing to guide and strengthen our hearts and minds. Through the Holy Spirit's leading, we may embrace and develop these gifts in order to leave behind the ugliness of our broken past and experience the beauty and fullness of knowing Jesus. Seven mature swans are the perfect symbol of what it means to become mature and complete through the Holy Spirit's leading.

Even as the current year ends, our true love's generosity continues. From the relationship he made possible through Jesus and the cross through the invitation to enjoy a personal relationship with Jesus through the Gospels, the magnitude of our accumulating gifts leaves us struggling for words. Our true love's latest gift reaches even beyond us by inviting us to serve and bless others under the leading of the Holy Spirit. And yet, some of the best gifts remain unwrapped. Tomorrow, our true love plans to bless us in eight new and wonderful ways.

January 1

Eight Maids a Milking
The Beatitudes – Blessings for God's People

On the eighth day of Christmas, my true love gave to me ...
Eight maids a milking,
Seven swans a swimming, six geese a laying,
Five golden rings,
Four calling birds, three French hens,
Two turtledoves, and a partridge in a pear tree.

Happy New Year! Today we celebrate "newness." From the Rose Bowl, with its parade and jet fly-overs, to the Winter Classic in hockey, big things are taking place. New Year's Day is also a day to celebrate small things, however. We are always curious to learn when the first baby born this year will arrive. I am still fascinated when twins are born a few minutes apart, but in separate years. How much confusion will that create later in life?

New Year's Day is the day when we all start over. It offers hope. It offers opportunity. We simply resolve to be better.

And when it comes to making resolutions, we are not shy. We resolve to improve our physical, emotional, financial, and spiritual well-being, all at the same time! Our intentions are sincere and the year is still too new for our willpower to have been seriously challenged. Today is a good day because our goals are still on track.

Our true love's eighth gift connects the ideas of making resolutions and living a blessed life. The gift of eight maids busily engaged in the process of milking cows calls to mind an image of great abundance. When "The Twelve Days of Christmas" was written, a family owning just one cow would be considered rich. Our true love's gift of eight productive cows is an extravagant gift that demonstrates overwhelming good fortune and prosperity.

Our true love's eighth gift is not just a description of being blessed, however. It is also symbolic of a collection of eight resolutions given to us by Jesus himself. Unlike the resolutions we typically make each year, Jesus's resolutions cause us to fundamentally rethink who we are. They challenge us to be better people and to enjoy the blessings that result from this transformation. Building upon the foundation of the budding relationship we have with Jesus as a result of our previous gifts, these resolutions—known as the Beatitudes—describe the best attitudes for life. Offered at the very beginning of the Sermon on the Mount, the Beatitudes (Matt. 5:3–12) encourage us to think and act like Jesus.

Blessed are the poor in spirit, for theirs is the kingdom of heaven.

No one enjoys being in the company of an arrogant person. Name-dropping, exaggeration, bragging, and self-promotion are unattractive characteristics, to say the least. Arrogant people often have a very unrealistic impression of themselves. They are not nearly as great as they think.

In contrast to an arrogant attitude, Jesus explains that genuine happiness flows from having an accurate understanding of ourselves. Our self-identities must be realistic. They have to be grounded in fact.

So when we say that someone is "poor in spirit," it does not mean that person is sad or depressed. Emotions are not the correct standard for measuring whether we are poor in spirit. Jesus is offering a contrast between something that is lower and something that is higher. In another context, we may say that someone has "poor judgment" as opposed to "good judgment."

A poor-spirited person recognizes that, while he has a relationship with God, he is not equal to God. This seems easy enough in theory, but living our lives in such a way that we do not pretend to be God is actually much more difficult. How often do we make important decisions without prayer? Do we ever judge what someone does, says, or looks like without knowing the full story? It is so easy to pretend to be God.

The first beatitude invites us to properly understand our relationship to God so we may become part of his heavenly kingdom. When we acknowledge that God is greater than we are, we are able to let go of the worries and anxieties that arise from thinking we always know best. Instead of relying on ourselves, we begin to rely upon God.

Blessed are those who mourn, for they will be comforted.

People often read this beatitude and mistakenly believe that God enjoys watching them suffer. Nothing is further from the truth. The second beatitude has to be understood in the context of the first beatitude if we want it to make sense.

The first beatitude asks us to humbly acknowledge our relationship to God. We then realize how impossible it is for us to even approach God's presence. He is perfect, and we are very imperfect. Being part of God's kingdom is only possible because God looks past our sins. This divine act of compassion on God's part is the comfort of which the second beatitude speaks.

When we have genuine sorrow for the sins in our lives, it results in equally genuine mourning. There is no joy that comes from thinking about all the areas of our lives in which we have failed. Yet God steps in and offers us the comfort that our sins will be forgotten if we have faith that his promises are true and that he has the power necessary to save us. The apostle Paul writes about this type of righteous mourning in 2 Corinthians 7:10: "Godly sorrow brings repentance that leads to salvation and leaves no regret."

Mourning is the appropriate response to realizing our spiritual helplessness. We are comforted, however, by Jesus's death on the cross and resurrection from the grave. This is God's perfect response to our heartache.

Blessed are the meek, for they will inherit the earth.

When we have a correct relationship with God and know he will forgive our sins, we gain a tremendous sense of confidence. We are at ease even when the world around us seems to be falling apart. In such circumstances, our gentle nature may cause people to question why we are so calm and collected. Nothing fazes us. What people are seeing is meekness or, stated another way, controlled strength.

John Dickson tells the story of three young men who mercilessly taunted a slightly older gentleman who was sitting quietly on the back of a bus in Detroit in the 1930s. When taunts failed to provoke the man, the bullies became more aggressive. Finally, the older gentleman arrived at his destination and started walking down the aisle of the bus toward the door, giving the youths his business card as he passed. It said, "Joe Louis, Boxer." On that day, the greatest characteristic of the future heavyweight boxing champion of the world was not physical strength, but restraint. Joe Louis personified meekness.

The world is full of people fighting for position, manipulating people, and bullying those whom they perceive as weak. Such behaviors are futile and pointless. When the most aggressive, manipulative bully goes to his grave, who mourns for him? Compare that bully to the person who lives a life characterized by meekness, who touches the lives of others by encouraging peace and patience. The meek inherit the earth by enriching us through their example and inspiring others to discover the source of their confidence. Their legacies last well beyond their lifetimes.

Blessed are those who hunger and thirst for righteousness, for they will be filled.

Hunger and thirst are powerful instincts. Babies want to put everything in their mouths, and the desire to consume only grows as we age. Instead of just food and drink, we also begin to consume products, concepts, and ideas. We even refer to people simply as "consumers," and an entire industry of marketing experts and advertising agencies spend billions of dollars trying to predict and influence what we desire to consume.

The fourth beatitude is not a call to abstain from our natural desires but rather a challenge to consider the nature and priority of those desires. Jesus is pointing us toward a deeper subject than physical nourishment. We are to seek righteousness first.

Righteousness is the product of living in accordance with God's will. Seeking righteousness stands in stark contrast to all the other things we crave in life. Those who hunger and thirst for popularity find that it lasts about five minutes in today's culture. Those who hunger and thirst for money find its value is uncertain and that wealth causes new worries. Those who hunger and thirst for power find that someone is always looking to knock them off the ladder of success. The Rolling Stones make fun of such self-indulgence in their famous lyric, "I can't get no satisfaction."

The fourth beatitude is not a promise of wealth, health, popularity, or power. What Jesus offers is the true satisfaction that comes from living life well and harboring no regrets.

Paul expresses this thought in Philippians 4:12-13. "I know what it is to be in need, and I know what it is to have plenty. I have learned the secret of being content in any and every situation whether well fed or hungry, whether living in plenty or in want. I can do everything through him who gives me strength." When we eagerly desire righteousness, we will be filled. Our other desires will then naturally fall into their proper place.

Blessed are the merciful, for they will be shown mercy.

It is hard to forgive others for the things they have done to us even when we know that Jesus's life and death were acts of God's mercy toward us. It is a challenge to show mercy to everyone in the same way that God has shown mercy to us, especially when they do not deserve it.

Showing mercy to those undeserving of mercy is one of God's most endearing and enduring characteristics, however. The parable of the unmerciful servant ends with the rhetorical question, "Shouldn't you have had mercy on your fellow servant just as I had on you?" (Matt. 18:33). Begrudgingly, we have to admit the answer is "yes." That means we cannot be bitter toward others while professing our love for Jesus. Such an attitude is an act of self-deception. As the prophet Micah explained, "He has showed you, O man, what is good. And what does the LORD require of you? To act justly and to love mercy and to walk humbly with your God" (Mic. 6:8). To understand the extent of God's mercy, the fifth beatitude indicates we must extend God's mercy to others.

Blessed are the pure in heart, for they will see God.

Sin spoils what is pure. Job identifies the fundamental problem with sin this way: "Who can bring what is pure from the impure? No one!" (Job 14:4). If the word of God ended with Job, there would be little point in Jesus giving the sixth beatitude. No one's heart is pure enough to see God.

To understand this beatitude, we need to know that even though God sees all of our imperfections, he is still willing to look past our sins. Just as an artist sees a stunning sunset instead of a blank canvas before picking up her brush, the Creator of the universe always sees the potential that resides within us.

King David was compelled to face the magnitude of his adulterous and murderous ways. In the midst of that crisis, he somehow retained the presence of mind to plead, "Create in me a pure heart, O God, and renew a steadfast spirit within me" (Ps. 51:10). This is no song of praise from a man casually worshipping God on Sunday morning. This is the desperate cry from a sinner drowning in the swirling currents of lust, adultery, lies, cruelty, hypocrisy, and murder. David knew if his heart was going to be purified, God was the only one who could do it.

Thankfully, God is willing to answer David's prayer in each of our lives. Paul prays "that your love may abound more and more in knowledge and depth of insight, so that you may be able to discern what is best and may be pure and blameless until the day of Christ, filled with the fruit of righteousness that comes through Jesus Christ—the glory and praise of God" (Phil. 1:9–11). As we become more like Jesus, we see God. He is working in our lives.

Blessed are the peacemakers, for they will be called sons of God.

Do you find it ironic that "Peacemaker" is the name given to a revolver and that whenever a country sends "peacekeepers" to trouble spots around the globe, they are usually heavily armed? The number of conflicts in the world seems to be growing by the day.

Giving peace was Jesus's purpose in life. The prophet Isaiah foretold how God will "judge between the nations and settle disputes for many peoples. They will beat their swords into plowshares and their spears into pruning hooks. Nation will not take up sword against nation, nor will they train for war anymore" (Isa. 2:4). Atheists frequently point to the endless conflicts that rage around the world and conclude that Jesus must have been a fraud. They misunderstand that the peace offered by Jesus is not just about global harmony. Oh, heaven help us if it is so limited!

Jesus's peacemaking mission focuses upon the conflict that rages within our hearts. That conflict is fought upon the battle lines of envy, pride, and selfishness. Jesus gives us the opportunity to end this conflict by accepting the peace he offers: "Peace I leave with you; my peace I give you. I do not give to you as the world gives. Do not let your hearts be troubled and do not be afraid" (John 14:27).

We share in this peacemaking mission when we are told to "go and make disciples of all nations" (Matt. 28:19). Paul even describes this work as "the ministry of reconciliation" (2 Cor. 5:18). As we help others find peace and end the conflict within their own hearts, we are doing the work of God's children. We are acting like Jesus Christ.

Blessed are those who are persecuted because of righteousness, for theirs is the kingdom of heaven.

Paul is the poster child for persecution in the name of Jesus. He was beaten, stoned, chained, whipped, chased, imprisoned, ridiculed, threatened, and chastised. Undaunted by those sufferings, he survived sleepless nights and days without food or drink, shipwrecks and snake bites, riots, challenges to his authority by his critics, and quarrelling among his friends. What would ever possess a person to accept such a life willingly and, as crazy as it sounds, gladly?

Faith. At the time of Jesus's ministry, Paul's faith was based upon the traditions of his ancestors. Paul was "extremely zealous" (Gal. 1:14) for the customs of his heritage and lived a lifestyle characterized by the pursuit of self-righteousness (Eph. 3:6). Paul gladly accepted the task of killing Christians because he believed they were undermining the spiritual authority of his mentors.

Paul's faith changed in a flash. Jesus's appearance to Paul blinded the killer's eyes, but opened the door to his heart. But in the decades of awesome ministry that followed, Paul was always acutely aware of his past. It clung to him like a shadow. It haunted him.

Still, Paul discovered that God's love is so wide and so long and so high and so deep that it easily surpassed the bounds of his own knowledge and experience. He realized that the persecutions he endured in Jesus's name were not a payback for his own sins but rather an unparalleled opportunity to exhibit the Gospel to his persecutors.

> Now I want you to know, brothers, that what has happened to me has really served to advance the gospel. As a result, it has become clear throughout the whole palace guard and to everyone else that I am in chains for Christ. Because of my chains, most of the brothers in the Lord have been encouraged to speak the word of God more courageously and fearlessly. (Phil. 1:12–14)

The final beatitude foreshadows the life of all who have suffered for their faith in Jesus. Too often we shy away from persecution, even in its mildest forms, because we desire to be liked or left alone. Paul's example gives us the confidence to recognize that even the stiffest form of persecution still provides an opportunity to share God's love with others.

Reflection

Adopting the lifestyle described in the Beatitudes is a worthwhile resolution. By living these attitudes, we grow much deeper in our relationship to Jesus. The Beatitudes also challenge us to live a more satisfying and meaningful life. This is the perfect gift for New Year's Day.

Our true love's outpouring of love and encouragement is mind-boggling. We do not deserve any of the gifts we have been given, but there they are. We now have eight amazing gifts that highlight our true love's overwhelming generosity. It all seems too good to be true. By now, we are almost desperate to share our good fortune with others.

Which, as you might have guessed, our true love already knows. Tomorrow's gift is given to us, but it is intended to be shared with others. It is like a big basket of fruit that we could never devour by ourselves. Our true love's ninth gift is yours to open, but it is to be shared with everyone. It is a family gift.

January 2

Nine Ladies Dancing
The Fruit of the Spirit – Blessings from God's People

On the ninth day of Christmas, my true love gave to me ...
Nine ladies dancing,
Eight maids a milking, seven swans a swimming, six geese a laying
Five golden rings
Four calling birds, three French hens,
Two turtledoves, and a partridge in a pear tree.

The merriment of Christmas and New Year's Day fades to the reality that the holidays are over on the ninth day of Christmas. The pre-holiday routines begin to resume. Depending upon how today falls on the calendar, this may be the first day back to work or the first day back to school. If not today, then those rituals of life are not too far off.

Contrary to what you may have assumed, our true love's gift of nine ladies dancing does not symbolize mothers rejoicing after dropping their cabin-fever afflicted children at school for the first time in weeks.

Today's gift of nine ladies dancing is symbolic of the fruit of the Spirit listed in Galatians 5:22–23. These nine character traits are so positive and universally recognized as good, it is inconceivable that anyone would oppose them. The fruit of the Spirit are also associated with the Holy Spirit, which connects today's gift with our last two presents.

The fruit of the Spirit are the visible evidence that the Holy Spirit is working in our lives. They are the tangible proof that we are obedient to Jesus Christ. By producing the fruit of the Spirit in our lives, many people are blessed by our actions and words. There is widespread rejoicing as God uses us to bless others. Thus, it comes as no surprise that ladies (and gentlemen) everywhere are dancing in jubilee when the fruit of the Spirit are present.

Love

The Bible may be summarized with just one word: love. Unsurprisingly then, the first fruit of the Spirit is love. From Genesis to Revelation, we read how God has loved us, how he currently loves us, and how he promises to love us in the future. Six days ago we saw why love is the greatest virtue of them all, and today our true love reminds us that God's love never fails.

The *agape* love we were given on the third day of Christmas is the same type of love that the Holy Spirit produces in us. *Agape* is firmly rooted in the will of the lover and not the loveliness of the object of our affection. It is an intentional love that knows no distinctions based upon race, gender, age, wealth, ethnicity, education, health, nationality, faith, or any other basis. *Agape* love perfectly reflects God's essence.

John describes God's love in John 3:16, one of the most well-known verses in the Bible. In 1 John 3:16, John tells us that Jesus is the personification of love: "This is how we know what love is: Jesus Christ laid down his life for us. And we ought to lay down our lives for our brothers." The next two verses put the concept of loving others in practical terms: "If anyone has material possessions and sees his brother in need but has no pity on him, how can the love of God be in him? Dear children, let us not love with words or tongue but with actions and in truth" (1 John 3:17–18).

The power of this passage was vividly illustrated for me once while leading my adult Sunday School class. During our prayer time, one of our most faithful class members expressed a concern that his family's only vehicle was in the garage, that he could not afford the repair bill, and that he was in danger of losing his job because he lacked transportation. I was so much "in the zone" of teaching that I failed to connect that particular prayer request with one of the key passages for that very week's lesson. In 1 Corinthians 8:1–5, Paul commended the Macedonians' generous contribution to a special offering for famine relief even though they themselves were living in poverty.

Thankfully, in spite of my own inability to hear and acknowledge an important need right in front of me, three different people approached me after the class and said they felt convicted by the Holy Spirit to help our friend with his repair bill. That week, the class raised more than enough money to repair the car and some even lent their own vehicles to help our friend make his deliveries while the repairs were being completed.

Looking back, it was exciting to see how God's love was put into practice. It drew our class closer together as a group. I became more aware of the practical needs of others. We have the awesome privilege as Christians to take the perfect love that God has shown to us and replicate it in the lives of others. What a wonderful gift!

Joy

Joy is the second fruit of the Spirit. Joy is often mistaken for an emotion, when it really is an attitude. Emotions come and go quickly. They describe our perception of specific events at specific moments. By contrast, an attitude is bigger than any single situation and reflects our overall outlook on life. Having joy over a lifetime is far superior to simply being happy at any particular point in time.

The extent of a Christian's joy is directly related to the quality of his relationship to Jesus. Christ's birth is the foundation of our joy (Luke 2:10) and Jesus promises to share his joy with us (John 15:11). Later, he told the apostles that the temporary grief they would have when he was crucified would be replaced by a joyful attitude that could never be taken away from them following his resurrection (John 16:22).

Peter confirms that Jesus was correct. Peter described the resurrection of Jesus as filling us "with an inexpressible and glorious joy" (1 Peter 1:8). James even writes that we are to consider it "pure joy" whenever our faith is tested, because it is an opportunity to grow spiritually (James 1:2).

Joy is the antidote to worries and anxieties. It causes us to refocus our thoughts on Jesus, which puts our negative emotions in the proper perspective. Paul is emphatic that joy is crucial to letting the Holy Spirit work in our lives, writing, "Rejoice in the Lord always, I will say it again: Rejoice!" (Phil. 4:4).

Peace

The third fruit of the Spirit is peace. Peace is more than just the absence of conflict. It is the presence of God in our hearts. The Holy Spirit gives Christians peace in three important ways.

First, we have peace with God. In fact, peace is an attribute of God (2 Cor. 13:11; Phil. 4:9). Despite all the bad things we have done, God is willing—even eager—to forgive us. Through Jesus, God has already done the hard work that is necessary to make his forgiveness possible. As Paul writes in Romans 5:1, "we have peace with God through our Lord Jesus Christ, through whom we have gained access by faith into this grace in which we now stand."

Second, the Holy Spirit helps us live in peace with others. Paul encourages us to "[l]et the peace of Christ rule in your hearts, since as members of one body you were called to peace. And be thankful" (Col. 3:15). The writer of Hebrews encourages us to "[m]ake every effort to live in peace with all men" (Heb. 12:12). When we make peace with others, James 3:18 says we "raise a harvest of righteousness."

Finally, the Holy Spirit helps us find peace with ourselves. Paul prays that "the Lord of peace himself will give you peace at all times and in every way" (2 Thess. 3:16). Having the ability to live free of anxiety, doubt, and guilt is a gift from God.

Patience

Patience is the fourth fruit of the Spirit. When a child is told to be patient for just a few minutes, it feels like a death sentence. And many adults are even less patient than children. Today, products are ordered online and shipped directly to our door. Communication across continents is instantaneous. Meals are ordered and served in less time than it takes to sing "The Star Spangled Banner."

But for the most important things in life, it seems we always have to wait.

Patience is the result of seeing things from a broader perspective. When we think only about what is going on right here and right now, we miss the larger things that are taking place. James illustrates this when he talks about the patience of the farmer (James 5:7). If all we do day after day is stare at the crops we plant, we miss the spectacular sunrises and sunsets and storm clouds and sunbeams that make the harvest possible. Focusing upon what we want prevents us from seeing what God is doing.

Patience is learned by seeing things from God's perspective. Peter addresses this when he writes, "The Lord is not slow in keeping his promise, as some understand slowness. He is patient with you, not wanting anyone to perish, but everyone to come to repentance … Bear in mind that our Lord's patience means salvation" (2 Peter 3:9, 15). Thank goodness God is patient. If he was impatient like us, we would be in big trouble.

Patience lets us step back from the exact, precise moment we are living in to see the greater reality of God's will. From that perspective, we can endure anything just a little bit longer because we know God is working on our behalf (Rom. 8:28).

Kindness

Kindness is next. We all know at least one kind person. Often it is a relative or trusted friend. It may be someone who knows us really well—and loves us anyway.

The Old Testament describes God's kindness as "unfailing" (2 Sam. 22:31; Ps. 18:50) and "everlasting" (Isa. 54:8). In the New Testament, God's greatest act of kindness is fulfilling his promise to send Jesus as the perfect sacrifice for our sins. Paul even refers to Jesus as "kindness and love" in Titus 3:4–5a, where he writes, "But when the kindness and love of God our Savior appeared, he saved us, not because of righteous things we had done, but because of his mercy."

We imitate God's kindness by taking care of people's needs. Sometimes it is helping them through a divorce or a parenting crisis. Sometimes being kind is as simple as giving someone a much needed hug or encouraging word. James 1:27 and other passages challenge us to reach out to those who are afflicted, infected, disaffected, and rejected. We are to surround them with an embrace that defies human nature and logic. It is an embrace that originates within the kindness of the heart of God.

Generosity

The sixth fruit of the Spirit is generosity, which is sometimes translated as "goodness." It conveys the idea of meeting the material needs of others, even ahead of our own needs, and doing so eagerly. Doing good and being generous are linked together in the Bible. In 1 Timothy 6:18, Paul writes, "Command them to do good, to be rich in good deeds, and to be generous and willing to share." He tells the Galatians, "[t]herefore, as we have opportunity, let us do good to all people, especially to those who belong to the family of believers" (Gal. 6:10).

As we saw two days ago, generosity is also one of the gifts of the Holy Spirit. Being generous leads to two excellent outcomes. First, God is pleased because he "loves a cheerful giver" (2 Cor. 9:7b). Second, our offering will "result in thanksgiving to God" (2 Cor. 9:11b) from those who were the recipients of this generosity.

Thanks to the generosity of Christians through the centuries, we have hospitals, orphanages, schools, and universities. Generosity has led to the drilling of thousands of fresh-water wells, the distribution of millions of dollars of prescription drugs to those with diseases, and the provision of shelter and countless meals to the homeless and destitute. Christian generosity has significantly improved the quality of life for people of all nations.

By being generous, we discover that one of the greatest blessings in life is to meet someone else's needs. John Bunyan expressed this blessing in *The Pilgrim's Progress*: "A man there was, though some did count him mad,/The more he [gave] away, the more he had."

Faithfulness

Faithfulness is the seventh fruit of the Spirit. You might have read *Horton Hatches the Egg* as a child. Horton the elephant is tricked into making a promise that costs him greatly. He has to sit on an egg until it hatches, while the egg's irresponsible parent frolics away. Horton's faithfulness earns him the ridicule and insults of virtually everyone, but his answer is always the same: "I meant what I said, and I said what I meant. An elephant's faithful, one hundred percent!"

Our faithfulness to God is the focal point of Jesus's Parable of the Talents in Matthew 25:14–30. The master (God) went away on a trip and entrusted his servants (us) with the task of managing his valuables (God's blessings) while he was gone. Two servants were diligent and multiplied the master's valuables while he was away.

A third servant, however, chose not to be faithful. Instead of using the valuables and growing them, he secretly hoped he alone would enjoy them. He buried them in a place that only he knew about. Upon the master's return, the unfaithful servant's scheme was revealed and his unfaithfulness was punished.

The lesson is that God entrusts us with gifts that will bless others. When we try to hoard God's blessings, we are not exhibiting the traits of a faithful servant. The unfaithful Christian desires God's gifts but despises God. When we are faithful to God, the blessings he gives us should grow, multiply, and bless others as well.

Gentleness

The eighth fruit of the Spirit is gentleness. One of the highest compliments we can pay to a person is to refer to him as a "gentle soul." Gentleness combines the benefits of perspective, sensitivity, and mercy. It results from a person who is in a position of strength but voluntarily yields to the wishes or needs of someone who is weaker or undeserving.

Jesus referred to himself as being "gentle and humble in heart" (Matt. 11:29). Though he was God, he nevertheless followed his own teaching to "turn the other cheek" when his opponents wronged him (Matt. 5:33–42). Jesus accepted insults, whippings, and crucifixion while praying that these acts of cruelty would not be held again his accusers. He is the perfect example of gentleness.

The Holy Spirit produces gentleness in the lives of Christians. Paul encourages us by writing, "Let your gentleness be evident to all. The Lord is near" (Phil. 4:2). Elsewhere, in Ephesians 4:2, he writes that we should "[b]e completely humble and gentle; be patient, bearing with one another in love."

Refraining from doing something that is justified under the circumstances is very difficult. But Jesus demonstrates that it can be done. When we are gentle, people see the Holy Spirit working within us.

Self-Control

The final fruit of the Spirit is self-control. Children often find it difficult to be self-controlled. They instinctively reach for something new and attractive, regardless of whether it is a lollipop or a steak knife. As adults, we know it can be hard to resist the urge to satisfy our impulses.

Ironically, the person who writes the most about self-control in the New Testament is Peter, the apostle who often acted rashly and impulsively. Peter accumulated wisdom over the years. So when he writes that self-control helps us prepare mentally for the challenges of life and helps us focus upon God's grace (1 Peter 1:13), we can be confident he is correct. When he tells us that self-control improves our prayers (1 Peter 4:7), we believe him.

Self-control is the opposite of selfishness. In terms of our relationships with others, it means we are intentional and attentive. We do not take people for granted. We show them respect, and we look for opportunities to help them.

To be self-controlled, however, we first have to be self-aware. Both 1 Thessalonians 5:6 and 1 Peter 5:8 associate self-control with being alert to what is going on around us spiritually. Are we aware when other people are suffering emotionally? Do we know what it looks like when someone is thirsting for truth? How do we recognize a stronghold of evil in a person's life? When we see the world as God sees it, we become more self-controlled.

Reflection

The nine fruits of the Spirit describe our ideal attitudes, thoughts, and instincts. They also reflect God's character as we allow the Holy Spirit to use us to enrich the lives of others. Thus, our true love's gift of nine ladies dancing for joy is a good symbol for the outpouring of the Holy Spirit. The fruits of the Spirit create a carnival of Christ-likeness.

Nine days have passed this Christmas season, and there are three days yet to come. It seems impossible that our true love's generosity is not yet exhausted. What more could we possibly hope for?

As the tenth day of Christmas nears, rest assured that our true love's generosity is not waning. His last three gifts are just as amazing as those we have already received. They are pointing us to even greater things. Tomorrow's gift will be especially liberating. I guarantee it.

January 3

Ten Lords a Leaping
The Ten Commandments – Freedom
through Grace

On the tenth day of Christmas, my true love gave to me ...
Ten lords a leaping,
Nine ladies dancing, eight maids a milking,
Seven swans a swimming, six geese a laying,
Five golden rings,
Four calling birds, three French hens,
Two turtledoves, and a partridge in a pear tree.

The first week of the year is a depressing time for many. Credit card bills and tax forms start arriving in the mail. The daylight hours are short. Memorial Day is five months away. The magic of the holidays is gone. If today happens to be a Monday, well, that's the quadruple whammy. Some folks label the first Monday in January as "the most depressing day of the year."

In keeping with the theme of putting aside the fun of the holidays and getting refocused on our routines, our true love's gift for today is, no joke, ten rules. Hurray! The leaping lords of the tenth day of Christmas are symbolic of the Ten Commandments, which God gave to guide the actions of the nation of Israel in the Old Testament.

As we recall from history, noble lords exercise authority over the common people. They dictate what is acceptable within their realm. They rule. So the natural question is whether our true love's tenth gift is an indication that our blossoming relationship with Jesus is about to be ruined by a strict requirement to obey a rigid set of rules. Not at all.

From "The Twelve Days of Christmas," we know that these particular ten lords are leaping. Lords do not normally leap. Spontaneous displays of fun are well beneath the dignity of the landed gentry. Only someone with much greater authority could make a single lord leap. Only the highest authority—a king, for instance—could make ten lords leap. It seems our true love is telling us that the Ten Commandments are themselves subject to the will of someone possessing the highest power and authority.

This is our true love's real gift. While rules and commandments do a great job of pointing out our failures in life, the Ten Commandments are not the standard by which our eternal destinies are determined. If our fates rested upon keeping the Ten Commandments perfectly, we would all be doomed. Thankfully, God's grace is more powerful than any rules, and that grace frees us from the condemnation that the law always has hanging right over our heads. God allows us to escape the punishment we deserve for our sins.

Here is the amazing thing. It is precisely because of our growing relationship to Jesus that the Ten Commandments no longer have any authority to condemn us. These ten lords are leaping out of the way as we run to embrace our Savior, Jesus Christ, the King of all kings.

With this insight in mind, the Ten Commandments assume their proper role and purpose in our lives. They point us in the direction of having a healthy relationship with God and others, but they also remain subject to God's sovereign judgment and mercy. The Ten Commandments are like road signs that direct us toward God's grace. They demonstrate just how dependent we are upon God.

The First Commandment
You shall have no other gods before me.

Ancient cultures worshipped the sun, the moon, stars, rocks, trees, animals, kings—you name it. The desire to put our faith in some greater power is nearly universal. Even today, people often put their faith in money, influence, success, fame, beauty, and youth. All of these things are temporary.

The question posed by the first commandment is not whether we will acknowledge God's existence, but whether we will put him at the top of our priority list. Is our relationship with God so important to us that everything else is less significant? Instinctively, we say yes. Actually living our lives so that our words and actions confirm this answer is much more difficult, however.

God knows that when we make our relationship with him our top priority, we will quickly see that he is the only person in whom we would ever want to put our faith. The first commandment challenges us to examine our priorities and motivations. If we are unwilling to make God the true Lord of life, then we are left to chase after things that are temporary and unfulfilling.

The Second Commandment
You shall not make for yourself an idol in the form of anything in heaven above or on the earth beneath or in the water below.

Idols come in two forms. Sometimes we worship a false god (1 Kings 16:30–33). Other times we worship the true God falsely (1 Kings 12:25–31). Both types of idolatry are prohibited.

Worshipping an idol of a god that does not exist is just plain silly. The worshipper is placing faith in something that does not really exist. The prophet Habakkuk outright mocks those who worship an object carved from a piece of wood or metal (Hab. 2:18–20). It is waste of time.

Likewise, worshipping an idol that is supposed to represent the true and only God is also a mistake. God cannot be confined to any single object or image. He is too great and too powerful. God is simply too big to be captured in any object of worship.

There is no shortage of things we idolize in today's culture. Even Christians sometimes fall prey to the idea that we can manipulate God by how we describe him and represent him. The second commandment asks us to consider where our hearts' desires truly lie. Do we want a genuine relationship with the Creator of the universe, or are we simply looking for a good-luck charm?

The Third Commandment
You shall not misuse the name of the LORD your God.

Certain words and phrases come to mind when we think of using God's name in vain. Unfortunately, God's name is associated with some of the most prolific cursing we ever hear. The swearer rarely even thinks about what he is saying. The use of God's name in a curse, outburst, or swearing fit is inconsistent with his holy character and nature. It is disrespectful. We should not do it.

But does the commandment go further? Consider this example. Do we ever criticize someone else in God's name? Have Christians ever waved a pointed "holier than thou" finger at someone? Making judgments about others is the new American pastime, it seems. The third commandment suggests we should let God speak for himself and not be in any rush to condemn others on his behalf. We should be cautious about speaking rashly on God's behalf when it is not our place to do so.

The Fourth Commandment
Remember the Sabbath day by keeping it holy.

The fourth commandment reminds us that the seventh day of the week is already holy. When God completed all of his work in creation, he rested (Gen. 2:3–4). For a nation coming out of slavery in Egypt, the fourth commandment would have been wonderful. It gave them one twenty-four hour period each week to rest. It also gave the Israelites time to assemble and reflect upon God's work on their behalf (Lev. 23:3).

We might not think of rest as being a gift from God, but it is. After burning the candle at both ends for much of the Christmas season, being reminded to rest is welcome advice. Jesus wants us to relax. In Matthew 11:28, he says, "Come to me, all you who are weary and burdened, and I will give you rest. Take my yoke upon you and learn from me, for I am gentle and humble in heart, and you will find rest for your souls. For my yoke is easy and my burden is light."

When we share our burdens with God, it is an opportunity to step outside the hassles, anxieties, and frustrations of life to think about his love, provision, and concern for our well-being. Rest is a blessing that recharges our bodies while filling our souls with God's presence.

The Fifth Commandment
Honor your father and mother, so that you may live long in the land the Lord your God is giving you.

We generally associate the fifth commandment with young children who are told they must be obedient to their parents. Have you ever noticed, though, that there is no age limit for this commandment? Could it be that the duty to honor your father and mother applies regardless of whether you are four or fifty-four? The command to honor our mature parents may be even more practical and challenging than telling a young child to simply do as he is told.

The command to be respectful to those who are older seems outdated in an era where youth is celebrated. Ignoring or being disrespectful of those who are older causes us to miss out on the wisdom they can share, however. Honoring parents means we submit our desires and needs to theirs, giving them respect on the basis of their status regardless of whether that respect is merited.

The Sixth Commandment
You shall not murder.

Only men and women were created in the image of God (Gen. 1:26; Gen. 9:6). Therefore, human life is very valuable.

Nevertheless, the world is filled with hatred and rage. The internet and television are filled with stories of murder and other crimes of malice. Sadly, the desire to settle disputes by killing someone is as old as the story of Cain and Abel.

King David illustrates this peculiar aspect of human nature. Despite having the perfect opportunity to assassinate King Saul and make himself king of Israel, David spared Saul's life (1 Sam. 24:3–7). However, a few years later, David callously ordered his best general to assure the death in battle of one of his most brave and loyal soldiers in order to cover up an adulterous affair (2 Sam. 11). David's example points out the startling reality that everyone is capable of anything under the right circumstances.

Anticipating this, Jesus taught that the best way to control ourselves is to control our thoughts. In Matthew 5:22a, he says, "But I tell you that anyone who is angry with his brother will be subject to judgment." In other words, by not quickly seeking a resolution to conflicts, we only set ourselves up for more conflict.

The Seventh Commandment
You shall not commit adultery.

The seventh commandment preserves the integrity of marriage, promotes a stable home environment, and encourages the emotional and spiritual growth of our children. Marriage is ordained and established by God as part of the creation (Gen. 2:24). As such, its sacred nature is to be respected by the husband and wife and others.

God is also concerned with protecting his relationship with us. As we saw earlier, the relationship between God and his people is often described as a marriage. The story of the prophet Hosea is one example. Even though Hosea's wife is unfaithful, he still loves her, accepts her, and cares for her. God does the same thing for us. Even when we sin and are unfaithful to him, he is still ready to take us back and love us as if we had never disobeyed him. The story of the lost son in Luke 15:11–32 tells the same tale. The Bible is filled with reminders that God loves us, no matter what we have done.

The Eighth Commandment
You shall not steal.

The prohibition against stealing is so self-evidently good that it seems almost incredible that it has actually had to be written down, right? Wrong. People steal things all the time—whether by taking someone else's property, cheating on their taxes, or simply by depriving someone of something that is rightfully theirs.

The eighth commandment shows the extent to which God is concerned with our relationships with others. When Christians steal from anyone, we are setting a very poor example of how our relationship with Jesus has changed the direction of our lives. Honesty is a character trait that reveals itself over time, and, often, in small ways or situations that are not always obvious. By contrast, dishonesty quickly destroys the goodwill and reputation we have earned. If we are to be the "light of the world" (Matt. 5:14–16), we must be known for our honesty.

The Ninth Commandment
You shall not give false testimony against your neighbor.

The command to speak truthfully in official matters is a foundation of civilization. Without it, there would be no ability to seek or bring about justice. With good reason, the ninth commandment is generally understood and often translated simply as "do not lie," a broader admonition that is equally meritorious. The overall discouragement of other "talking" sins such as slander and gossip would also appear to be in mind.

Although the tongue is a small part of the body, it has the ability to get us into a disproportionate amount of trouble. Words can never be unspoken. We can only apologize for them. James 3:1–12 explores the ways in which the things we say can both praise God and bring down curses. The ability to communicate is a wonderful blessing, but we must be careful what we say. We should always be mindful of the ways in which our words impact the lives of others and our relationship to God.

The Tenth Commandment
You shall not covet your neighbor's house. You shall not covet your neighbor's wife, or his manservant or maidservant, his ox or donkey, or anything that belongs to your neighbor.

The last commandment is a collection of several related prohibitions all having one thing in common. While adultery, murder, theft, and lying are all behaviors that involve actions noticeable by others, coveting takes place within the confines of our own minds. Only God knows when we secretly want someone's spouse, home, clothes, jewelry, gadgets, or car.

The commandment against desiring what belongs to others goes to the root of our sinful nature. Even before we sin, we have a wicked desire. The tenth commandment tells us to avoid dwelling on such thoughts since that is the best way to prevent our evil desires from developing into sinful acts (James 1:13–15). The point is sobering. God's commandments extend beyond what we actually do or say, but also to what we think.

The Purpose of the Ten Commandments

Concluding the Ten Commandments with a rule against dwelling on evil thoughts is a bitter pill to swallow. Even if we have never openly disrespected our parents, killed or robbed someone, committed adultery, or lied about something, we all have had the very strong desire to do so at one point or another. It is impossible to obey all of the Ten Commandments every single day of our lives.

Ultimately, the purpose of the Ten Commandments is not to create obstacles that prevent us from having a genuine, personal relationship with God. Quite to the contrary, they demonstrate that the closest possible relationship with God is not made possible by our ability to obey rules. We can't be perfect. Instead, the source of our freedom is God's willingness to overlook the many times we have already been disobedient.

The Ten Commandments help us realize we need a Savior. Paul writes in Romans 3:21, "But now a righteousness from God, apart from the law, has been made known, to which the Law and Prophets testify." In other words, the Old Testament proves that our only hope for having a good relationship with God must come from God's grace, and not from our own ability to follow his rules perfectly. Hebrews describes the Old Testament as "only a shadow" of the better covenant established by God's grace (Heb. 10:1).

The New Testament points out that Jesus came to earth to fulfill the Old Testament law (Matt. 5:17). In so doing, he made it obsolete (Heb. 8:13; Rom. 8:1–2; Rom. 10:4). When Jesus was asked to pick which of the commandments was the greatest, instead of picking one of the Ten Commandments, he gave a new command: "Love the Lord your God with all your heart and with all your soul and with all your mind. This is the first and greatest commandment" (Matt. 22:37–38). To amplify the point, Paul writes in Romans 13:10b, "Love is the fulfillment of the law."

God's grace and mercy allow us to live in his presence despite our sins. Paul writes in Galatians 3:24, "So the law was put in charge to lead us to Christ that we might be justified by faith. Now that faith has come, we are no longer under the supervision of the law." The Ten Commandments are a vivid reminder of the scope and depth of God's love for us.

Reflection

God's grace is the true gift given on the tenth day of Christmas. The Ten Commandments did not bring people one step closer to God. They simply served as a constant reminder of just how far apart from him our sins make us. The Ten Commandments have no power to determine whether we spend eternity in God's presence. That decision has already been given to us through the greatest gift of all, Jesus Christ.

What began as a dull day filled with post-holiday blues has become an opportunity to reflect upon God's grace. He has saved us from ourselves. Our true love wants to make certain we know this.

With two days left to go this Christmas, we wonder what our true love might possibly have left to give. The answer, as we shall see, is awesome. Tomorrow's gift shows us that the relationship we are forming with Jesus has already taken root and blossomed in the lives of others. They are a wonderful example of God's grace in action.

January 4

Eleven Pipers Piping
The Apostles – Examples of
Faithfulness

On the eleventh day of Christmas, my true love gave to me ...
Eleven pipers piping,
Ten lords a leaping, nine ladies dancing,
Eight maids a milking, seven swans a swimming, six geese a laying,
Five golden rings,
Four calling birds, three French hens,
Two turtledoves, and a partridge in a pear tree.

Did you notice the daylight seemed to last just a little longer today? By the eleventh day of Christmas, the winter solstice (the shortest day of the year) is now two weeks behind us. That means there has been an extra minute or so of daylight each day. The increase is barely noticeable from one day to the next, but the addition of almost twenty minutes of daylight over the last two weeks is perceptible.

When Jesus was born, the Roman Empire celebrated the feast of *Sol Invictus* (the "unconquerable sun") at the winter solstice to herald a new season that brings light. To counter these misguided pagan festivities, Christian leaders in the fourth century decided to celebrate Jesus's birthday on December 25. Although we do not know the exact date of Jesus's birthday, Christians would now be able to celebrate their own "unconquerable Son."

Our true love's gift of eleven pipers piping also signals the arrival of a new season of light. A single piper belting out a tune will draw attention and attract a crowd in no time flat, but eleven pipers piping are enough for a parade. That is exactly what our true love has in mind.

Our true love's eleven pipers are symbolic of Jesus's apostles. Though Jesus chose twelve apostles, Judas Iscariot eventually betrayed him. Our true love's focus is upon the remaining eleven apostles who stayed with Jesus throughout his ministry. Following his return to heaven, these men would carry the gospel far and wide and build up the church as the community of Jesus's followers. The apostles were like pipers leading joyful parades of good news across three continents. Their stories, as well as the stories of other faithful Christians through the centuries, are inspiring to us. That inspiration and encouragement is our true love's real gift on the eleventh day of Christmas.

Eleven Apostles

When I think of the apostles who followed Jesus, I cannot help but think of the movie *The Bad News Bears*. If you have seen the movie, you will recall that the Bears were a Little League team that had no reasonable chance at amounting to much on the field. Only through a degree of coercion could a coach be found, and he was no Yogi Berra. Despite the many problems they faced, the Bears eventually came together to form a winning team.

By any objective standard, the original band of brothers that Jesus assembled was also anything but a well-oiled machine. John MacArthur's biography of the apostles is accurately entitled *Twelve Ordinary Men*. Not one of the apostles was recognized as a natural leader, nor were any of them titans of business, celebrities, or scholars. There is a good chance that if you lined all of them up in a row, it would have been difficult to choose the one "most likely to succeed." The apostles blended in as part of their local communities as if they were part of the scenery itself.

Peter, Andrew, James, and John

Peter and Andrew were brothers, as were James and John. All four of these men were fisherman and business partners (Luke 5:10), working their trade in the backwaters of the Sea of Galilee. These men were familiar with the teaching of John the Baptist and were on the lookout for the Christ. When John the Baptist identified Jesus as "the Lamb of God" (John 1:36), the fishermen were eager to get to know him better.

Their early acquaintance with Jesus allowed them to be present at many of the key moments in his ministry. They witnessed events that the other apostles missed, and they asked Jesus some of the most important questions about the kingdom of God. Their relationship with Jesus enabled them to become some of the most visible and outspoken leaders of the early church.

But following Jesus was costly. James was the first apostle to be killed for his faith in Jesus. Peter and John influenced and authored several books in the New Testament, but Peter was eventually crucified and John was forced into a harsh exile. Despite this, these four apostles continue to inspire us through their writings and example.

Phillip and Nathaniel

Jesus next invited Phillip and his friend Nathaniel (also called Bartholomew) to join him (John 1:43). Phillip's willingness to follow Jesus was likely due to an acquaintance with Peter and Andrew, who were from the same small town. Although Nathaniel initially doubted Phillip's claim that Jesus could be the Christ, Jesus miraculously revealed his divine nature by reciting Nathaniel's recent activities and then reading his mind. Jesus's reputation and actions clearly demonstrated he was a man worth knowing.

Still, there is little about Phillip or Nathaniel that stands out in the New Testament. Their primary qualification for becoming Jesus's disciples appears to have been their strong desire to see the God's plan fulfilled and their willingness to follow a man who spoke with authority and performed miracles. Because of their hopes, availability, and curiosity, Phillip and Nathaniel became trusted friends of Jesus and continued his ministry.

Matthew and Simon the Zealot

Matthew (also called Levi) joined Jesus's party a little later. A tax collector serving as an agent of the Roman government, Matthew was despised by his Hebrew countrymen as a sinner and a traitor. Matthew was no fool, though. As we learned a week ago, his gospel was written from the standpoint of one who was knowledgeable and respectful of the traditions and prophecies of his ancestors. Matthew's decision to leave the lucrative tax collection business was triggered in part by Jesus's controversial willingness to have dinner at Matthew's home. Jesus even used the occasion to criticize the self-righteous religious leaders who thought Jesus's association with Matthew was scandalous (Luke 5:29–32).

From Matthew's perspective, Jesus was the Christ because he was everything the religious leaders were not. Jesus was sincere, genuine, loving, compassionate, knowledgeable, powerful, and, most importantly, the fulfillment of each Old Testament prophecy concerning the coming Christ. Though he was a social outcast, Matthew recognized Jesus as the Christ.

On the other end of the political spectrum, we have Simon. The most notable fact about Simon was his association with a group of Israelites committed to overthrowing the Roman government in Palestine. While we do not know the circumstances of Simon's invitation to join Jesus, his recruitment certainly cast Jesus in a negative light to the Romans and the Jewish leaders.

When Jesus was wrongfully accused of trying to lead a rebellion against Rome and establish a new kingdom, his friendship with Simon may have been part of the evidence used against him. If Jesus was interested in protecting his "brand" as a good teacher, he would have avoided having Simon the Zealot as a student. The fact that Simon was one of the original apostles further demonstrates that Jesus's purpose was to reach everyone, and that a person's politics are of no account in the kingdom of God.

What would it have been like for Matthew and Simon to sit down at their first campfire together? It is easy to imagine the arguments they might have engaged in over politics and culture, but it is also likely that these two outcasts (though for very different reasons) could find common ground in their unenviable social status. The only person who accepted them as they were was a young teacher from Nazareth. Jesus brought them together to serve in a new kingdom that was far greater than anything they could have possibly imagined. The kingdom of God was open to everyone.

Thomas, Thaddaeus, and James, the son of Alphaeus

We do not know anything about the circumstances under which Thomas, Thaddaeus (also called Judas, the son of James, and not to be confused with Judas Iscariot), and James, the son of Alphaeus, came to be apostles of Jesus. When these three apostles are mentioned in the Gospels, it is often just in passing.

We often think of Thomas as the "doubter," but John's Gospel portrays him as bravely being willing to go to Jerusalem with Jesus even if it meant he would die (John 11:16). Thaddeus plays no major role in the Gospel stories. His only mention comes when he asks a question during the Last Supper (John 14:22). Even less is known about James, the son of Alphaeus. He is never specifically quoted or identified in any New Testament story. From a brief mention in Mark 15–16, we learn his mother was one of Jesus's followers and was with the women who first found the empty tomb.

Though they did not write any letters that we know of and they were not always present at the key moments of Jesus's ministry, these apostles nevertheless shared a role in the greatest story of all time. They remind us of the numerous Christians we know who have faithfully served Jesus without ever being singled out for praise.

One Mission

The apostles followed Jesus throughout his ministry and later carried on his work. Their commitment to this mission unquestionably resulted from their experiences, conversations, and observations. Their perspectives and attitudes were shaped by the teaching, miracles, and actions of a man whom they often misunderstood or, at times, even feared. Yet it was the act of following Jesus that enabled them to see that what they had been given was much more significant than a series of lectures in philosophy or morality. The apostles were uniquely offered an invitation to participate directly in the fulfillment of God's plan for saving the world.

The enormous magnitude of this invitation probably dawned on each of them gradually and not necessarily at the same time. The Gospels record how Jesus prepared these men for the mission he would soon be giving them. Before there was a Great Commission (Matt. 28:18–20) or a miraculous appearance of the Holy Spirit on the day of Pentecost (Acts 2), there were opportunities to grow as individuals and learn what it meant to follow Jesus.

First Steps

On one occasion, Jesus sent the apostles on a short preaching tour of Israel. In Matthew 10, he tells them to proclaim a simple message,

"The kingdom of heaven is near" (Matt. 10:7). The plan was not very bold. It did not involve detailed outlines of theological nuance nor did it come with promises of riches and glory for those who accepted the message. The point was simple: "The Christ is here. Tell someone!"

The results of the trip were amazing. In Mark 6, we read how the apostles gathered around Jesus after reuniting from their journeys. Just like young children recounting a day's adventure to their father, the apostles told about the miracles they had performed and the excited reactions of the Israelites when they heard the news that the kingdom of God was at hand.

Next Steps

Jesus commissioned the apostles for an even greater task on the night before his death. He spoke plainly about the events that were soon to follow and what those events would mean for the eleven.

First, Jesus demonstrated the attitude of humility and service they must possess by washing their feet. "I tell you the truth, no servant is greater than his master, nor is a messenger greater than the one who sent him" (John 13:16).

He then told them that the best evidence of their commitment to him would be the extent to which they followed his example. "A new command I give you: Love one another. As I have loved you, so you must love one another. By this all men will know that you are my disciples, if you love one another" (John 13:34–35).

He assured the apostles that his death and resurrection would announce the beginning of a new era. The apostles' miracles and ministry would even surpass what Jesus had accomplished in three years. "I tell you the truth, anyone who has faith in me will do what I have been doing. He will do even greater things than these, because I am going to the Father" (John 14:12).

Jesus also encouraged the apostles by telling them that they would never be alone. "And I will ask the Father, and he will give you another Counselor to be with you forever—the Spirit of truth ... But the Counselor, the Holy Spirit, whom the Father will send in my name, will teach you all things and will remind you of everything I have said to you" (John 14:16–17a, 20).

Jesus's transparency during the Last Supper is so apparent. He held nothing back, even telling his apostles that they too would be insulted, persecuted, hated, and killed. Nevertheless, their mission must be completed. "And you also must testify, for you have been with me from the beginning" (John 15:27). Seeing the fear, uncertainty, and anxiety on the faces of his apostles, Jesus comforted them:

> I tell you the truth, you will weep and mourn while the world rejoices. You will grieve, but your grief will turn to joy. A woman giving birth to a child has pain because her time has come; but when her baby is born she forgets the anguish because of her joy that a child is born into the world. So with you: Now is your time of grief, but I will see you again and you will rejoice, and no one will take away your joy.
> (John 16:20–22)

Then Jesus prayed. He prayed that the apostles would be protected and enabled by their own spiritual growth to be living examples of his teaching.

Final Steps

Jesus appeared to the apostles on several occasions after his resurrection. The last of these appearances was on a hill in Galilee not far from where their journey with Jesus began just three years before. Jesus's Great Commission (Matt. 28:18–20) challenged the apostles to take the gospel to all nations, making disciples of Jesus

Christ as they went, through baptism and by teaching the world the beauty and power of *agape* love. It was the commencement address at the apostles' graduation ceremony. After spending three years with Jesus, the apostles were ready to continue his ministry.

Although the Bible tells us very little of what became of many of these apostles, early church historians tell us they obeyed Jesus's command and took the gospel message far and wide. The travels and works of the apostles are preserved in various locations and traditions from England to India and Russia to Ethiopia. Their work throughout the Roman Empire, alongside the work of Paul and others, is well documented in the New Testament. Many of them willingly paid the ultimate price for their allegiance to Jesus.

Our Inspiration

The most remarkable part of Jesus's prayer on the night of his arrest is that he also prayed for us. Though separated in time from his prayer by nearly two thousand years, we were at the forefront of Jesus's thoughts. He prayed that the unity he shared with God and the Holy Spirit would be shared and joined by all who would accept the invitation to be his friend. Amen to that prayer.

What inspired the apostles to travel and share the gospel continues to inspire. It led a man named Patrick to take the message of Jesus to the pagans in Ireland. It emboldened William Wilberforce to speak out against the injustice of slavery and end the practice throughout the British Empire. It inspired a man named David Livingstone to travel the rivers of Africa proclaiming the gospel. It opened the eyes of a businessman named George Williams to the need for a place where young men could receive spiritual guidance and direction, causing him to establish the Young Men's Christian Association. It led a young woman to travel to India and open orphanages and hospices under her assumed name, Theresa of Calcutta. It has led people to translate the Bible into hundreds of languages and to lovingly serve others in parishes, hospitals, schools, jails, and slums. We could go on and on and on. We have a proud heritage as Christians. It is a heritage built on the foundation of the apostles' example as Jesus's earliest disciples.

Reflection

The apostles' legacy of faithfulness is shared with us today. Their inspiration fuels our pursuit of one common mission—to imitate God's goodness by helping others become Jesus's disciples. Today's gift from our true love reminds us we are not alone in that effort.

When we greet someone, serve them, or embrace them in Jesus's name, we stand in the same company of a multitude of saints who have preceded us. The church began with people who lacked any apparent qualifications to lead a worldwide evangelistic crusade, yet they saw in Jesus the answer to all their greatest questions, needs, and hopes. The apostles' example continues to lead a parade of nations who worship Jesus.

With one day left in the Christmas season, the gathering of God's people is exactly what our true love has in mind. Tomorrow's gift may bring this year's Christmas celebration to a close, but it anticipates a greater celebration that will never end.

January 5

Twelve Drummers Drumming
Heaven – The Promise Fulfilled

On the twelfth day of Christmas, my true love gave to me ...
Twelve drummers drumming,
Eleven pipers piping,
Ten lords a leaping, nine ladies dancing,
Eight maids a milking, seven swans a swimming, six geese a laying,
Five golden rings,
Four calling birds, three French hens,
Two turtledoves, and a partridge in a pear tree.

"Christmas is almost over."

Two weeks ago, we might have said that with a little bit of hopefulness in our voice. The arrival of Christmas Day would signal that the end was in sight. We were close to getting past all the hard work that goes into the holiday season, if we could just hold out a little longer.

Today, however, the statement strikes a little different chord. Instead of looking forward to Christmas coming to an end, we hate to see it go. Our true love's gifts over the past eleven days have opened our eyes to what Christmas really means for us. He has demonstrated, time and time again, that the celebration of Christmas is about so much more than presents, or a tree or decorations. Christmas is about our relationship to God.

The great temptation on the twelfth and final day of Christmas is to look backward. We are naturally inclined to reflect upon what has already happened rather than on what comes next. Our memories of Christmas—especially this year—are just too precious to simply put away.

Our true love's twelfth gift, however, is not a photo album. Although he has already blessed us beyond our wildest imagination, he is not looking backward. Our true love's focus is squarely on what still lies ahead. Today's gift is twelve drummers pounding out a rhythm that commands attention and brings all other activity to a standstill. It is the loudest gift of them all, surpassing the calling birds, the French hens, and even the pipers piping. Everyone stops to watch a drum line. The loudest, boldest, and most ostentatious gift of the Christmas season is coming.

So what do twelve drummers symbolize? What future event are they ushering into our presence? Long before we can even fully see it, we know that this gift is very special.

We look ahead, certainly, to Easter, which celebrates the resurrection of Jesus Christ. But Easter is an annual commemoration of a historical event that has already taken place. The drummers do not symbolize Easter. We also look forward to next Christmas, when we will once again celebrate Jesus's birth. But that is not the purpose of the drummers either.

The twelve drummers symbolize the thing we look forward to most. It is an event that is the fulfillment of God's promise to us. It is the Day of the Lord, the day when every knee bows and every tongue confesses that Jesus Christ is the Lord of all. It is the promise of that glorious day that is given on the twelfth day of Christmas. The crescendo that has been building on each day of this Christmas season is ready to come to fruition in a climax that proves our relationship with Jesus is genuine and authentic. As with all of our gifts from our true love, both the number of drummers and the task in which they are engaged symbolically represent our true love's final gift—living in God's presence.

Heaven

The number twelve is used frequently in the Bible to describe something that is important. For instance, there were twelve tribes of Israel. When Joshua crossed the Jordan River and entered the Promised Land, he erected an altar of twelve stones taken from the river (Josh. 4:20). Likewise, Elijah used a similar twelve-stone altar to demonstrate the supremacy of God over the gods of Baal (2 Kings 18:31). You get the gold star if you recall that the first temple in Jerusalem had a bronze altar in the courtyard that rested upon twelve bronze bulls (1 Kings 7:25). Throughout the Old Testament, the number twelve is associated with that which belongs to God, particularly his people.

In the New Testament, we remember that Jesus called twelve apostles. Jesus was himself twelve years old when he first amazed people with his understanding of God (Luke 2:42, 47). When Jesus finished feeding the crowd in Galilee, how many baskets of food were left over? You guessed it, twelve (Luke 9:17). Jesus's trip to restore the life of Jairus's twelve-year-old daughter is interrupted by a woman who touches the hem of Jesus's cloak and is miraculously healed after having a medical condition for twelve years (Matt. 9:20–22). The number twelve figures very prominently in Jesus's ministry and miracles.

The greatest concentration of "twelves" in the Bible, however, is found in Revelation 21–22, where John describes heaven. Here we see that heaven has "a great, high wall with twelve gates." Each gate is fashioned from a single pearl and inscribed with the name of one of the twelve tribes of Israel (Rev. 21:12). The wall itself is placed upon twelve foundations, with each of them bearing the name of one of the apostles. The dimensions of heaven are all multiples of twelve. Within heaven, the tree of life—not seen since the fall of man in Genesis 3—reappears and once again brings forth its fruit in twelve annual crops (Rev. 22:2). Heaven's magnificent attractions are emphasized by the repeated use of the number twelve. The fact that heaven is our true love's final gift is also emphasized in the nature of the twelve drummers' actions. They are not just standing around. They are drumming. Loudly. The Olympic opening ceremony offers the slightest hint of what it will be like to live in heaven. At the Olympics, we see athletes from around the world entering the stadium in a celebration of peace and unity. They celebrate unique cultures and heritages while coming together under one common banner. But we also know the Olympics provide nothing more than a temporary distraction from the conflicts that otherwise rage across the globe. The Olympic opening ceremony is an incomplete, human conception of a divine ideal of the perfect community.

The parade of nations John describes in Revelation is far superior. There are no prejudices, inequities, or favoritism to disrupt its unity. The richness of diverse cultures, languages, eras, and experiences weave together a tapestry of humanity that is unified and blessed. The people in Revelation praise God and serve one another in an environment that can only be described as perfect. There is no conflict. There is no darkness. There is no sickness. There are no tears. There is no sin. There is no death. It is heaven.

John explains the nature of our eternal home in Revelation 21:22–7 and 22:3–5:

> I did not see a temple in the city, because the Lord God Almighty and the Lamb are its temple. The city does not need the sun or the moon to shine on it, for the glory of God gives it light, and the Lamb is its lamp. The nations will walk by its light, and the kings of the earth will bring their splendor into it. On no day will its gates ever be shut, for there will be no night there. The glory and honor of the

nations will be brought into it. Nothing impure will ever enter it, nor will anyone who does what is shameful or deceitful, but only those whose names are written in the Lamb's book of life ... No longer will there be any curse. The throne of God and of the Lamb will be in the city, and his servants will serve him. They will see his face, and his name will be on their foreheads. There will be no more night. They will not need the light of a lamp or the light of the sun, for the Lord God will give them light. And they will reign for ever and ever.

Life everlasting in the presence of God! This is our true love's gift on the twelfth day of Christmas. Whether we realize it or not, living in God's presence has been the purpose behind every other gift we have received from our true love. The image of twelve drummers leading God's people in a triumphant procession through the twelve gates of heaven is a powerful picture. The twelfth day of Christmas anticipates this glorious event. As Christians, we look forward to being united with the entire community of Christ's followers and living in the eternal presence of God. This is the ultimate prize for accepting our true love's invitation to have a close and personal relationship with Jesus.

Reflection

Even before the creation of the universe, God desired to have a personal relationship with each of us. Though sin complicated his efforts to build this relationship, God was always working to accomplish his will. He succeeded, even though it meant Jesus had to die on the cross.

The kingdom of God is real. It is here. It lives in our hearts just as much as it exists in heaven. The task of reconciling the world to God is already fully underway.

We are blessed to share in the legacy of prior generations of believers who imitated Jesus by giving *agape* love to others. Now it is our turn. Even as we go about this world-changing mission, we eagerly anticipate the day when we will realize the fulfillment of God's supreme promise. The relationship he always desired with us is still available to us.

The twelfth day of Christmas brings the Christmas season to a conclusion for another year. But the purpose, meaning, and effect of Christmas should never be far from our thoughts. Our true love has demonstrated generosity beyond anything we could ever have hoped for, but we still don't know his name. Who is our true love?

Conclusion

Who is My True Love?

You can tell a lot about a person by the gifts they give. Is the person generous or stingy? Does the person give with no expectation of repayment, or does the gift come with strings attached? Is the person's generosity scheduled and rigid, or does it occur spontaneously? How much thought did the person put into the gift? What sacrifice did the person make in order to make the gift possible? When we receive a gift, we learn quite a bit about the giver.

Throughout "The Twelve Days of Christmas," our focus is on the true love's gifts. And what a lavish display of giving we see. On the first day of Christmas, our true love gave the gift of a Savior. Jesus gave up the privileges of heaven so that he could come to earth, walk the same dirty streets we walk, and, ultimately, undo the work of Satan by reversing the curses of sin. The purpose behind the first gift of the Christmas season finds its fulfillment in our true love's final gift. On the twelfth day of Christmas, our true love gave us the gift of spending eternity in God's presence, surrounded by his people.

In between theses bookends of the Christmas season, our true love has given us gifts that highlight God's goodness. The Bible's two covenants tell the story of God's work on behalf of humanity in all of its magnificence. The three virtues of faith, hope, and love offer us the opportunity to live a good life. The four Gospels invite us into a closer relationship with Jesus, only to be followed by a precious reminder from the five books of the Pentateuch that God keeps his promises. With the six days of creation, we see that God is powerful enough to do everything he promised.

Our true love's emphasis shifts to our response to God's work beginning on the seventh day of Christmas. The seven gifts of the Holy Spirit help us mature in our faith. The eight Beatitudes describe the attitudes that best characterize a healthy Christian lifestyle. The nine fruits of the Spirit illustrate the many ways in which we bless others as a result of our relationship to Jesus. The Ten Commandments remind us that God's grace is so great that even our worst offenses may be forgiven and forgotten. The eleven apostles inspire us with their courage, boldness, and commitment to Christ. In all of these gifts, our true love reminds us of Jesus while pointing us toward heaven.

No finer collection of gifts has ever been given anywhere at any point in human history. Our true love's generosity is unmatched. His gifts are given freely to anyone who will accept them. They were costly to him, but they are free to us. They are the product of his own will to share. They are not given out of guilt or obligation. The gifts are exquisite. They possess value that is both timeless and timely. They are proof that God knows us better than we even know ourselves and that he sincerely cares for our needs. They convince us that his desire to know us and enjoy spending time with us is genuine.

What is so easy to miss in "The Twelve Days of Christmas," however, is the fact that the song is not really about gifts at all. First and foremost, the song is about love. True love. As hard as it may be to think of this, the 364 gifts given over a twelve-day period are simply a way of expressing the very essence of the gift giver's nature. By now, there is no doubt that only God himself could give gifts such as this. There is simply no one who is capable of doing so much on our behalf.

"The Twelve Days of Christmas" reveals that God is our true

love. He is real and sincere. When all the other things the world has to offer are finally discarded as false, our true love will still be true.

Several centuries ago, someone was wise and creative enough to compose a song and lyrics that capture the majesty of God's essence, his plan for humanity, and his desire to know us as his children. That carol has been preserved and handed down from one generation to the next ever since. It has been sung in churches, in schools, in offices, in factories, in homes, in cars, on street corners, in hospitals, and on the radio. Ironically, many people sing it without any awareness of the profound truths expressed in the song's rich symbols and images. The unknown composer would be extremely pleased to know that the message of his lyric is still alive and well today.

But "The Twelve Days of Christmas" still holds one last mystery. Only you can solve it.

It is easy to overlook the fact that this Christmas carol is written from a very specific point of view. "The Twelve Days of Christmas" is a heartfelt song written by someone who knew firsthand what God has done. It is written from a very personal perspective. It is, after all, a song about the generosity of "my" true love. And by adding that simple two-letter word, the composer cuts to the heart of the questions about all that we believe about faith and life and love. The composer's position is clear. God is his true love.

Is the same statement true for us? Is "The Twelve Days of Christmas" still just a whimsical rhythm of absurd generosity, or has its meaning grown to the point where we also may sing it as our personal anthem about the love God has personally shown us? That question is one that we each must answer in our own way and in our own time. By drawing us time and time again to the love of God on each day of the Christmas season, the composer of "The Twelve Days of Christmas" has given us his own unique gift. Thank you.

It is my sincere hope that this Christmas season ends happily. For those who accepted Jesus Christ as their Lord and Savior long ago, "The Twelve Days of Christmas" affirms the foundations of our faith and inspires us to pursue our relationship with our true love even more eagerly in the New Year. The song transforms the Christmas season into an annual reminder that our spiritual growth is inevitably leading us toward something greater and bigger than ourselves.

For those whose faith in God is just now blossoming, "The Twelve Days of Christmas" is one of many ways to spur the process of spiritual growth. Each day of the Christmas season offers new insights into God's love. Each of these gifts challenges us to explore, consider, and worship God's nature. Take the time to go back and read each of the scriptures we have studied and consider how God is calling you into a deeper relationship.

Finally, for those whose faith in God is nonexistent or uncertain, "The Twelve Days of Christmas" is an invitation to experience his power and grace. We are not expected to accept these gifts and blessings on blind faith alone. God welcomes our questions, our doubts, our fears, and our anxieties because they give him the opportunity to demonstrate the trueness of his love. If you are open to considering and accepting God for who he claims to be, by all means, pursue the blessings and promises and proofs that have been offered to you over the past twelve days. Let them spur your curiosity and eagerness to know our true love. Let God pursue you and bless you in the same way a proud and loving father dotes over his children.

As for me, I never imagined that a book about God's essence would spring from what I thought was a silly Christmas song. Yet, the process of discovering and describing the blessings offered in "The Twelve Days of Christmas" has been exciting and liberating. I can say, without reservation or qualification, that God is my true love. I can sing "The Twelve Days of Christmas" more boldly and proudly than ever precisely because I now understand its true meaning. That, in and of itself, is a blessing and one I hope we share.

Merry Christmas!

Postscript

Keep Christmas Well, All Year Long

The singular goal behind writing and publishing *My True Love's Gifts* is to inspire others to rediscover God's love. We all want to be used by God in such a way that we leave things better than we found them and, in the process, be worthy of the title of a "good and faithful servant." That is the essence of Charles Dickens's parting passage in *A Christmas Carol*, which is quoted at the beginning of this book. Ebenezer Scrooge's life was so transformed that the postscript of his life was this: "And it was always said of him, that he knew how to keep Christmas well, if any man alive possessed the knowledge. May that be truly said of us, and all of us!" Now that we know our true love, the challenge is to keep Christmas well all year long.

There are many ministries and missions around the world that do a wonderful job of blessing others every day—most often in ways that never gain the attention they deserve. By purchasing *My True Love's Gifts*, you have already supported some of these ministries because one hundred percent of the net proceeds from the sale of the book will be contributed to these and other Spirit-led organizations:

YOU CHOOSE

www.youchoose.community

YOUCHOOSE is an internet community that engages people with short, culturally relevant biblical videos that people will enjoy, like, share, and connect with. Based in Northern California, YOUCHOOSE challenges people to connect with Christ using a simple church format that is as trendy as Silicon Valley and as timeless as the first-century church. YOUCHOOSE uses videos and social media to help people dive deep into what it means to follow Jesus as well as what it means to be a disciple who makes disciples. By emphasizing how the church is a community and not a building, YOUCHOOSE is empowering a new generation to connect and reconnect with Christ.

Refuge for Women is a nonprofit, faith-based organization that provides long-term care for women who have escaped human trafficking or sexual exploitation. With locations in several cities across the United States, Refuge for Women offers up to twelve months

www.refugeforwomen.org

of safe housing and healing with twenty-four-hour-a-day staffing. The ministry's trained and compassionate staff helps residents reclaim their own identities and assists them in reaching goals to overcome addictions, develop life skills, and achieve spiritual, financial, and emotional independence. Refuge for Women strives to help each woman complete the program and leave the ministry with a vision for her future, equipped to succeed and sustain a life marked with dignity and hope. This growing ministry is effective: 95 percent of the women who complete the Refuge for Women program have remained committed to their new lifestyle.

www.amohonline.org

Appalachia Mission of Hope is a Christian nonprofit organization that serves the Appalachian region of Kentucky from its headquarters near McKee, Kentucky. The goal of Appalachia Mission of Hope is to not only provide necessary aid to the people of Appalachia, but in doing so, to show God's love in action. In addition to sponsoring several events throughout the year, Appalachia Mission of Hope coordinates the distribution of clothing, household goods, small appliances, furniture, and food to many families in the Appalachian area through a network of partner churches and organizations throughout Eastern Kentucky. Appalachia Mission of Hope plants seeds that blossom into lasting, personal relationships with Jesus Christ.

www.ukcsf.org

Christian Student Fellowship is a nondenominational campus ministry at the University of Kentucky. It exists to live out and share the good news of Jesus Christ to people throughout the University of Kentucky community in a variety of ways: Midnight Pancakes, Bible studies, spring break trips, weekly worship services, and much more. Christian Student Fellowship is built around the belief that if we can change the campus, we can change the world. As a student at the University of Kentucky in the 1990s, I can personally attest to Christian Student Fellowship's life-changing purpose and mission.

I encourage you to learn more about the awesome work these ministries are doing and, if so led, to join in their efforts by volunteering, contributing, praying, or through other means.

Notes

Epigraph and Introduction

Charles Dickens closes out his ode to the spirit of Christmas with a favorable assessment of the reformed Ebenezer Scrooge. See *A Christmas Carol* (Dover Thrift Editions), Charles Dickens, Dover Publications, Mineola, NY (1991).

The symbolism within "The Twelve Days of Christmas" is the subject of both a children's book and scholarly studies. These texts include *The Real Twelve Days of Christmas*, Helen Haidle, Zonderkids, Grand Rapids, MI (1997); "The Twelve Days of Christmas," Hugh D. McKellar, *The Hymn*, Vol. 45, No. 4 (Oct. 1994); and *The New Oxford Book of Carols*, Hugh Keyte and Andrew Parrott, Ed., Oxford University Press (1992). Despite much speculation as to the origin of the song, there is currently no definitive documentation as to the identity of the composer of "The Twelve Days of Christmas," the date of its composition, or the composer's intentions in producing this great allegorical work.

December 25

The movie *How the Grinch Stole Christmas* was released on November 17, 2000. It was directed by Ron Howard and produced by Universal Pictures and Imagine Entertainment. "Where Are You Christmas?" was sung by Cindy Lou Who, portrayed by Taylor Momsen.

The meaning of the term "Christ" is taken from the *New*

Bible Dictionary, 3rd Ed., D.R.W. Wood, Editor, Intervarsity Press, Downers Grove, IL (1996) p. 576. For a more complete description of many Old Testament prophecies fulfilled by Jesus, I encourage the reader to consult chapter 8 of *The New Evidence that Demands a Verdict*, Josh McDowell, Thomas Nelson Publishers, Nashville, TN (1999).

The unique characteristics of the partridge, or *phasianinae*, as scientists would call it, are described in *The Sibley Guide to Bird Life and Behavior*, National Audubon Society, Chris Elphick, John B. Dunning, Jr. and David Allen Sibley (Ed.), Alfred A. Knopf, New York, NY (2001), pp. 233, 239.

December 26

The scriptures come alive as we put them in their appropriate historical, cultural, theological, and social context. The greatest resource I have discovered for doing this is the commentaries on the Old Testament and New Testament published by College Press in Joplin, Missouri. Any student of the Bible who desires to delve into God's Word should read and consider the College Press commentaries as part of their studies.

December 27

The story of how French hens were historically reserved for consumption by the noble classes of Europe is set forth in *The Real Twelve Days of Christmas*, Helen Haidle, Zonderkids, Grand Rapids, MI (1997).

Oswald Chambers penned an excellent work on understanding loss and doubt by examining the experience of Job in *Baffled to Fight Better*, Discovery House, Grand Rapids, MI (1982).

The movie *Chariots of Fire* was released in the United States on April 2, 1982, and earned four Oscar awards from the Academy for Motion Pictures, including best picture and best original screenplay. The movie was produced by Twentieth Century Fox Film Corporation and written by Colin Welland.

"All We Need Is Love (Christmas in the Yard)" was performed by Jamaican reggae singer Orville Richard Burrell, who is better known as Shaggy. The song was released on one of the best-selling Christmas albums of all time, *Now That's What I Call Christmas!* produced by Universal Music Group, Santa Monica, CA (2001).

The definitions of the Greek words *agape* and *phileo* are drawn from *Vine's Concise Dictionary of the Bible*, W.E. Vine, Thomas Nelson, Nashville, TN (1999), pp. 225–226. The dissimilar meaning of the Greek word *eros* is taken from *The Oxford Dictionary of the Christian Church*, F. L. Cross (Ed.), Oxford University Press, New York (1974), p. 839.

December 28

The corrupting nature of tax collection practices in the era of Jesus's ministry are described in James M. Freeman's *The New Manners and Customs of the Bible*, Bridge-Logos, Alachua, FL (1998).

Each of the College Press Commentaries on the New Testament's Gospels are excellent. For an in-depth understanding of the nuances of each of the Gospel writers, I recommend *Matthew*, Larry Chouinard, College Press, Joplin, MO (1997); *Mark*, Allen Black, College Press, Joplin, MO (1995); *Luke*, Mark C. Black, College Press, Joplin, MO (1996); *John*, Beauford H. Bryant and Mark S. Krause, College Press, Joplin, MO (1998), pp. 17, 37–38. Professor Mark E. Moore has done an excellent job of illustrating the richness of the Gospels, as well as presenting the history of Jesus's ministry in sequence, in a single user-friendly volume, *The Chronological Life of Christ*, College Press, Joplin, MO (2007).

December 29

The central role of the Sinai covenant set forth in Leviticus to the nation of Israel is described in *Leviticus—Numbers*, Clyde M. Woods and Justin M. Rogers, College Press, Joplin, MO (2006), pp. 24–26.

December 30

The deep theological message in Genesis is wonderfully explained in *Genesis*, Paul J. Kissling, College Press, Joplin, MO (2004). It is a must-read for anyone seeking to understand Genesis in its best historical, cultural, and spiritual context.

Professor Frank Wilczek won the 2004 Nobel Prize for physics. In *A Beautiful Question: Finding Nature's Deep Design*, Penguin Press, New York, NY (2015), he provides a historical survey of science's quest to understand the true essence of the universe. The book also provides a thoughtful meditation on the objective beauty nature has to offer through the work of the "Artist."

The transcendence of creation stories among all cultures and ethnicities is the subject of several informative works such as *Creation Myths of the World*, David A. Leeming, Ph.D. ABC-CLIO, Inc., Santa Barbara, CA (2009); *Flood Legends*, Charles Martin, Master Books, Green Forest, AR (2009); and *Myths from Mesopotamia: The Creation, the Flood, Gilgamesh, and Others*, Stephanie Dalley (Trans.), Oxford University Press, Inc., New York, NY (1989).

December 31

For more on cygnets and other classic children's stories, consider reading *Hans Christian Anderson's Complete Fairy Tales*, Jean Pierre Hersholt, (Trans.), Thunder Bay Press, San Diego, CA (2014).

George Barna describes disturbing survey results in an article entitled, "Most American Christians do not Believe that Satan or the Holy Spirit Exist," The Barna Group (April 10, 2009). One of the best evangelical surveys of biblical passages on the Holy Spirit is *The Holy Spirit: A Biblical Study*, College Press, Jack Cottrell, M. Div., Joplin, MO (2006).

The illustration of the apple to describe the nature of God is illustrated in *3 in 1: The Picture of God*, Joanne Marxhausen, Concordia Pub. House, St. Louis, MO (1973).

That it is the Christian's duty to "make disciples" is a line of reasoning meticulously developed and documented in the book,

Make Disciples, Terry A. Bowland, D. Min., College Press, Joplin, MO (1999).

John Greenleaf Whittier's poetry is available in many texts. The couplet I quote is found in his poem "Maud Muller," which is printed at length in *One Hundred Choice Selections*, Phineas Garrett, Ed., Penn Publishing Company, Philadelphia, PA (1897).

January 1

Professor Mark E. Moore's chronological commentary on the life of Christ offers a wonderful exposition of the Sermon on the Mount, including the Beatitudes. See *The Chronological Life of Christ*, Mark E. Moore, College Press, Joplin, MO (2007).

While self-esteem and self-perception are the subject of thousands of books and articles, some of the notable early works in the study of these subjects are *The Psychology of Self-Esteem*, Nathaniel Branden, Nash Publishing, Los Angeles, CA (1969) and *Feeling Good: The New Mood Therapy*, David D. Burns. M.D., Harper, William Morrow and Co., New York, NY (1980).

The Joe Louis story is recounted by John Dickson in *Humilitas: A Lost Key to Life, Love and Leadership* (Kindle Locations 192–202), Zondervan (June 7, 2011).

"I Can't Get No Satisfaction," the anthem of all who imitate Solomon's vain quest for fulfillment in life through materialism and sexual pleasure, was written and recorded by the Rolling Stones before being released by London Records on June 6, 1975.

For an extensive survey of the history of the Colt Single Action Army "Peacemaker," consult the two-volume *Colt Peacemaker Encyclopedia*, Keith Cochran, Cochran Publishing Company, Rapid City, SD (1992).

January 2

The quote on generosity comes from *The Pilgrim's Progress*, John Bunyan, Signet Classics, New American Library, Penguin Group, New York, NY (2009), p. 252.

Horton Hatches an Egg, Theodor Seuss Giesel (Dr. Seuss), Random House, New York, NY (1968) is a wonderful description of faithfulness, perseverance, and self-sacrifice.

January 3

The fact that the first Monday in January has become known as the "most depressing day of the year" is attested to in several media outlets. One that caught my eye is, "Feeling Glum? Well it is Blue Monday: Rain, debt and divorce make it worst day of the year," *The Daily Mail*, Sam Webb, Jan. 5, 2014 (http:www.dailymail.co.uk/news/article-2534162/Dont-expect-tomorrow-January-6-officially-depressing-day-year.html) (last visited Jan. 17, 2015).

For more information on the significance of the Ten Commandments, particularly with regard to the use of God's name and the reminder that the Sabbath day is already holy by the time of Israel's deliverance from Egypt, see *Exodus*, Randall C. Bailey, Collect Press, Joplin, MO (2007), pp. 220–222.

January 4

The history of the fourth-century practice of celebrating Christmas on December 25 of each year, in relation to the pagan *Sol Invictus* celebration, is recounted in works such as *Christianity, The First Three Thousand Years*, Diarmaid McCulloch, Viking Penguin Group, New York, NY, (2010) p. 200; and *The Oxford Companion to the Bible*, Bruce M. Metzger and Michael D. Coogan (Eds.), Oxford University Press, New York, NY (1993), pp. 112–13.

To see a team of "nobodies" that accomplished much more than expected, as Jesus's apostles did, watch *The Bad News Bears*, Paramount Pictures (1976).

For an easy to understand biography of each of the apostles, John MacArthur's *Twelve Ordinary Men*, W Publishing Group, Nashville, TN (2002), is a great resource.

About the Author

David Samford enjoys writing, and his favorite writing opportunities are those that tell people about the amazing, undeniable scope and depth of God's love and mercy. Though Samford's career as a law clerk, speechwriter, attorney, and Special Justice of the Kentucky Supreme Court has allowed him to write materials as diverse as the Kentucky Derby Trophy presentation, the State of the Commonwealth Address, and numerous legal briefs and opinions, it is God's loving generosity at Christmas that led him to publish his first book.

Samford's other passion is helping others, whether it is by teaching the game of basketball to elementary students, mentoring young professionals in the early phases of their careers, serving in various volunteer roles, helping clients through the complexities of government and politics, or simply leading a Bible study for most of the past seventeen years. Samford's insightful perspective and optimistic attitude are firmly rooted in his unshakable faith in God's goodness and faithfulness.

Samford is blessed to have a wife who enables him to pursue his dreams and two wonderful children who remind him of God's love each day. As Samford and his family continue their own journey with Christ, they hope to inspire others.

Samford would love to hear from you. Please connect with him through this book's website at www.mytruelovesgifts.com or on Facebook at www.facebook.com/MyTrueLovesGifts.